CATHOLICS IN AMERICA

RUSSELL SHAW

Catholics
in
America

*Religious Identity and
Cultural Assimilation
from John Carroll to
Flannery O'Connor*

IGNATIUS PRESS   SAN FRANCISCO

Cover:
Wikimedia Commons images
(from top to bottom)

Archbishop John Hughes
Library of Congress Prints and Photographs Division
Brady-Handy Photograph Collection

Orestes A. Brownson
Portrait by George Peter Alexander Healy (1863)
Museum of Fine Arts, Boston

Mother Frances Cabrini

Archbishop John Carroll
Painting by Rembrant Peale (1811)

James Cardinal Gibbons
(October 18, 1917)
Library of Congress Prints and Photographs Division

Flannery O'Connor
Photograph by Robie Macauley (October 9, 1947)

Cover design by Davin Carlson

ISBN 978-1-62164-143-8
Library of Congress Control Number 2014949942
Printed in the United States of America ∞

CONTENTS

INTRODUCTION

A Tale of Two Flags

In my parish church, as also, I suppose, in many another Catholic church in the United States, two flags are prominently displayed. One is the Stars and Stripes. The other, unfamiliar to most Americans, including many Catholics, is the gold and white flag of Vatican City, with the papal coat of arms—the keys of Peter and the papal tiara—imposed upon the vertical white band. In many churches, the two flags flank the sanctuary as if to salute the sacred ritual celebrated there. In mine, they hang from the choir loft at the back of the church, where they seem to be maintaining a benign surveillance of the congregation.

In all my years of visiting Catholic churches, I've never heard anyone, priest or layperson, say a word about the symbolism of the two flags, perhaps because it's so obvious that it doesn't need explaining. Their message plainly is twofold: first, that Catholics have a dual loyalty—to the Church and to the United States; second, that there is *no conflict here*. On the contrary, their reply to the ancient question, "Can you be a good Catholic and a good American?" appears to be an implied, "Who says I can't?"

For a long time, that response was entirely reasonable. It was the starting point and basis for the program of Americanization pursued by Catholic leaders from John Carroll onward. In the early years of the twentieth century,

Harvard philosopher George Santayana, a self-described "aesthetic Catholic", marveled that American Catholics busy assimilating into American culture could so happily embrace something so "profoundly hostile" to their faith.[1] Some years later, however, a letter dispatched to the Vatican by the princely George Cardinal Mundelein of Chicago offered an unusually candid explanation of why Catholic assimilation was not just reasonable but absolutely necessary.

Responding to an impassioned protest to Rome by Polish priests angered by his attempts to prevent Polish-born members of his Windy City flock from retaining their Polish cultural identity, with Catholicism central to it, Mundelein declared it of "the utmost importance" that nationality groups in America should "fuse into one homogeneous people ... imbued with the one harmonious national thought, sentiment and spirit." This, he told Rome, was "the idea of Americanization", and anything else would be "a disaster for the Catholic Church in the United States".[2]

For the most part, that has remained conventional wisdom to this day. Now, though, this may be changing. In recent years, it's become increasingly clear that the Church needs to rethink the old project of unconditional assimilation into American secular culture. Yes, assimilation has been the preferred strategy of Catholic leadership since John Carroll. But should it always be? A persuasive argument can be made that it needn't and shouldn't. For the cost of assimilation to the Church has grown unacceptably high as the secular culture has become ever more

[1] George Santayana, *Character and Opinion in the United States* (London: Constable, 1924), 47–48.

[2] Quoted in Jay P. Dolan, *In Search of an American Catholicism* (New York: Oxford University Press, 2002), 139–40.

inhospitable to Catholic beliefs and values, a process now observable on issues from abortion and same-sex marriage to the creeping economic strangulation of parochial schools. Currently the question has particular urgency in light of the presence in the United States of yet another large body of mainly Catholic newcomers: the Hispanics.

A while back I wrote a book called *American Church*, in which I discussed the problem of assimilation (the problem's nature is suggested by the book's subtitle: *The Remarkable Rise, Meteoric Fall, and Uncertain Future of Catholicism in America*). In laying out my thesis, I said this:

> As a sociological, psychological, and even spiritual process, Americanization was bound to happen. But it did not have to happen just as it did, nor must all the results now be accepted just as they stand.... Two linked questions become more and more pressing: How American—in contemporary American secular terms—can Catholics afford to become without compromising their Catholic identity; and must the future of Catholicism in the United States be more Americanization as we've experienced it up to now, or do we have other, better options?[3]

American Church was surprisingly well received, and the problem of assimilation received some badly needed attention as a result. I've even heard that some people who read the book have taken steps to carry out its practical prescription for the rebuilding of a viable U.S. Catholic subculture. *Catholics in America*—a collection of fifteen short profiles of people whose careers illustrate aspects of the phenomenon examined in *American Church*—is meant to encourage continued discussion. (Many of the

---

[3] Russell Shaw, *American Church: The Remarkable Rise, Meteoric Fall, and Uncertain Future of Catholicism in America* (San Francisco: Ignatius Press, 2013), 21.

profiles first appeared in slightly different form in the pages of *Our Sunday Visitor* newsweekly, to which I here extend thanks.)

This book can be read simply as a set of introductions to a group of individuals who in various ways made significant contributions to American Catholicism and American society. Readers are welcome to approach it that way if they wish. But they should be aware that a more complex rationale is at work here—the hope to stimulate an overdue dialogue on a question of great urgency in which they are invited to take part.

It's this: Can we still be fully Catholic while also being fully American in American secular terms? The response of many Catholics today is simply more assimilation into the values and behavior patterns of the society that surrounds them. But for a remnant of believing, practicing Catholics, it's a different story. These people find themselves increasingly alienated from the secular society and deeply concerned to know what to do about it. Perhaps they will find some help in what follows.

Several themes are at work here, exemplified by the following fifteen influential American Catholics: Archbishop Carroll and Cardinal Gibbons—the assimilation option as it has been accepted and promoted by leaders of the Church in the United States; Saint Elizabeth Seton, Father McGivney, and Al Smith—anti-Catholicism and the Catholic response; Archbishop Hughes and Saint Frances Xavier Cabrini—the immigrant experience; Cardinal Spellman—hyperpatriotism as an assimilation mode; Dorothy Day, Archbishop Sheen, Flannery O'Connor—the ambiguities of American culture; Orestes Brownson and Isaac Hecker—the feasibility of evangelization; John Kennedy and John Courtney Murray—resolving the tension between church and state.

Let me reply at the start to a possible objection: this is *not* an unpatriotic book. "My country, right or wrong"—words associated with the early nineteenth-century American naval hero Stephen Decatur and later repeated, with disastrous results, by Cardinal Spellman—expresses an unassailably correct sentiment, provided the sentiment is understood to be, "No matter how foolishly or unjustly my country may act, it's still my country." But this fundamental acknowledgment of national filiation does not excuse patriotic citizens from criticizing their country when it acts foolishly or unjustly, and trying their best to get the country to stop doing that. These things, too, are expressions of patriotism, indeed arguably more useful than blind acquiescence.

With the necessary amendments, much the same thing might also be said regarding loyal Catholics and their uneasy reaction to the Church's historic policy of assimilation.

More and more these days, I find myself thinking about these things as I kneel beneath the two flags in my church. Then I am tempted to take as my text words of another archbishop of Chicago, the late Francis Cardinal George, in a column in his diocesan newspaper that was widely cited and reprinted. Writing of the upsurge of anti-Catholicism in secularist America, he spoke of the "self-righteous voice of some members of the American establishment ... who regard themselves as 'progressive' and 'enlightened'." Then he said this:

> The inevitable result is a crisis of belief for many Catholics. Throughout history, when Catholics and other believers in revealed religion have been forced to choose between being taught by God or instructed by politicians, professors, editors of major newspapers and entertainers, many have opted to go along with the powers that be.... It takes

no moral courage to conform to government and social pressure. It takes a deep faith to "swim against the tide".[4]

The stories of fifteen remarkable women and men brought together here help explain how it is that today's American Catholics find themselves having to choose: Will they conform or will they fight?

[4] *Catholic New World*, October 21, 2014, http://www.catholicnewworld.com/cnwonline/2014/0907/cardinal.aspx.

ARCHBISHOP JOHN CARROLL
(1735–1815)

"Equal Rights of Citizenship"

As the Revolutionary War drew to a close and the thirteen former British colonies settled into the serious work of
becoming the United States, American Catholics faced an
obvious, urgent challenge: to win acceptance by their fellow Americans. Catholics in the new nation numbered only
about twenty-five thousand, with the largest concentrations
in Maryland and Pennsylvania. Few were rich or influential. Indeed, in many places they were objects of contempt,
suspicion, and persecution—hostile legacy of the European
religious wars of the seventeenth century, still virulently
alive in the New World.

In such circumstances, the choice of a leader for the
Church in America was of critical importance. Selecting a
man who was either headstrong or weak could have had
disastrous consequences for years to come. John Carroll—
first bishop, later first archbishop, in the United States—was
the right man in the right place at the right time for this
onerous, highly sensitive position.

The Holy See plainly knew what it was about in choosing Carroll. Member of a wealthy and respected Catholic family, recognized as belonging to America's political
and social elite, the archbishop-to-be was to prove notably

adept at building bridges with the non-Catholic world during a career that spanned more than three decades.

Along with persuading Protestants that Catholics also had a place in America, John Carroll had to tackle the mammoth task of building the infrastructure of the Church from scratch. In this, too, he proved remarkably successful. Truly, as John Adams, who was to be second president of the United States, once remarked of the young priest, here was "a gentleman of learning and abilities".[1]

He was born January 8, 1735, at his parents' plantation in Southern Maryland, the fourth of seven children. His older brother, Daniel, was one of only five men who signed both the Articles of Confederation and the U.S. Constitution. His cousin and lifelong friend, Charles Carroll of Carrollton, was the only Catholic signer of the Declaration of Independence and the first U.S. senator from Maryland. Following early studies in Maryland, young John and his cousin Charles were sent to French Flanders to study at the Jesuits' College of St. Omer, an institution established to accommodate the sons of well-to-do English-speaking Catholics who had no Catholic schools in their own countries. In 1753, aged eighteen, he entered the nearby Jesuit novitiate to undertake the lengthy preparation for becoming a priest of the Society of Jesus. He was ordained in 1771.

In the summer of 1773, Pope Clement XIV, under pressure from several Catholic monarchs with whom the Jesuits had tangled, issued a brief suppressing the Society. Carroll was shocked but, having no other choice, accepted the papal decree. (In later life, he would display a marked

---

[1] Biographical information in this sketch is drawn largely from James Hennessey, S.J., "An Eighteenth-Century Bishop: John Carroll of Baltimore", in *Patterns of Episcopal Leadership*, ed. Gerald P. Fogarty, S.J. (New York: Macmillan, 1989). Unless otherwise noted, quotations are from this source.

preference—which he acknowledged—for ex-Jesuits like himself in filling clerical posts in his sprawling American diocese.) Returning home in 1774, he did pastoral work near what is now Washington, D.C., and there established the colonies' first Catholic parish.

In 1776, the Continental Congress, by now in open conflict with the mother country, dispatched a mission to Canada in hopes of persuading the French Canadians to join the struggle against Great Britain. Its members were Benjamin Franklin; Samuel Chase, a signer of the Declaration of Independence and later justice of the Supreme Court; and Charles Carroll of Carrollton. Although not formally a member of the group, Father Carroll was asked to accompany it and agreed to do so. A priest's involvement, it was reasoned, would smooth the way with the Catholics of French Canada, but the odds against success were very high from the start.

The Quebec Act, voted by the British parliament in 1774, was specifically cited by the Continental Congress in the Declaration of Independence as one of the colonists' grievances against George III justifying their break with the mother country. Among other things, the Quebec Act guaranteed free exercise of religion to the French-speaking Catholics of Quebec—a step that aroused strong anti-Catholic feelings in the thirteen colonies to the south and was a large part of what the Declaration had in mind in denouncing the king for "abolishing the free System of English Laws in a neighbouring Province" by allowing Catholics to worship as they chose. The Continental Congress could hardly expect the Catholics of Quebec to join the struggle against Great Britain while it simultaneously denounced George III for accommodating Catholics in this manner. Not surprisingly, the mission to Canada failed. But even so, Carroll's role in it strengthened his image among the movers and shakers of his day as a trustworthy and capable man.

In 1784, Pope Pius VI appointed him ecclesiastical superior of the mission in the United States. This was the same Pius VI who fifteen years later would die in France as a prisoner of the French Revolution. (John Carroll, though a strong supporter of the American Revolution, was disgusted with the extremism and bloodthirsty violence of this French approach to regime change.)

In the letter to Carroll announcing his appointment, Lorenzo Cardinal Antonelli, prefect of Propaganda Fide— the Vatican's Congregation for the Propagation of the Faith, which was responsible for foreign missions—cited his "piety and zeal", then added this not insignificant comment: "It is known that your appointment will please and gratify many members of that republic [the United States], and especially Mr. Franklin, the eminent individual who represents the same republic at the court of the Most Christian King [the king of France]." Franklin had been consulted about the choice of Carroll and had put in a good word for his companion on the mission to Canada eight years before. France, it should be noted, was the new nation's most powerful ally at this time and had provided the Americans with decisive military assistance in the recent Revolutionary War.

Four years later, with authorization from Rome, the two dozen or so men who then composed the body of Catholic priests in the United States voted for a bishop. The result was predictable: Father Carroll was the overwhelming choice. Pius VI approved and named him the first bishop in the United States on November 6, 1789. His Diocese of Baltimore encompassed the entire territory of the thirteen states.

This way of choosing a bishop may seem unusual today, when selection by the pope is the norm, but it was common enough in the late eighteenth century, a time when direct papal appointment of bishops was rare and local clergy typically made the choice, subject to the pope's approval. Often, too, secular authorities controlled the process—something the American government declined to do from the start (although, as we've seen, Benjamin Franklin, U.S. minister to France, lent his support to the selection of Carroll as superior of the American mission). In later years, Bishop Carroll favored having a method like that used in his selection become standard practice in the United States. Although in this he had no success, his approach to choosing bishops reflected the balancing act that he found necessary on this and all other matters—on one hand, unshaken loyalty to the pope as the Church's indispensable principle of unity, and on the other, ever-present sensitivity to the reality that too much involvement by Rome in American affairs "would draw on our religion a heavy imputation from the government under which we live".

A similar sensitivity to the pastoral needs of the Catholic community can be seen in his support for a vernacular liturgy. Insistence on Latin, he remarked in 1787, may have been a reasonable response to "insulting and reproachful demands" for the vernacular by early Protestant reformers. But now, the twin problems of illiteracy among the laity and a shortage of liturgical books pointed to the conclusion that "to continue the practice of the Latin liturgy ... must be owing either to chimerical fears of innovation or to indolence and inattention." Nearly two hundred years would have to pass before Carroll's argument for a vernacular liturgy prevailed in the wake of Vatican Council II.

Consistent with this attitude, he also sought a native-born clergy for the Church in the United States. In 1789, with the aim of training "subjects capable of becoming useful members of the ministry", he founded the school that was to become Georgetown University. Two years later he brought French Sulpicians to Baltimore to establish a seminary there. But in the Carroll years the small body of Catholic priests in the United States was for the most part foreign-born. Many of these men were committed and effective, but the group also included a fair number of eccentrics and troublemakers whom no other bishop wanted—"a medley of clerical characters" their realistic but resigned ordinary called them, and a continuing thorn in his side.

Something similar might have been said of the lay trustees who in a number of places owned the property of parishes and claimed the authority to hire and fire their pastors. Archbishop Carroll dealt firmly with this situation, but trusteeism was to plague his successors throughout much of the nineteenth century.[2] Here is the historical source of the entrenched hierarchical resistance to giving significant authority to Catholic laypeople that has dogged the Catholic Church in America up to the present day.

In recognition of the rapid growth of the Church in the United States, Pope Pius VII in 1808 created four new American dioceses—Boston, New York, Philadelphia, and Bardstown, Kentucky (whose status as a diocese later was transferred to Louisville). Baltimore became the metropolitan archdiocese, and John Carroll was elevated to archbishop. Two years earlier, in Baltimore, he had laid the cornerstone of the first cathedral in the United States—the Cathedral of the Assumption, today a basilica. Benjamin Henry Latrobe, architect of the U.S. Capitol in Washington, was its designer. But Carroll did not live to

---

[2] Trusteeism is present when lay parishioners claim administrative powers and the right to choose or remove pastors on the basis of civil law.

see its completion. He died in Baltimore on December 3, 1815, and is buried in his cathedral's crypt.

John Carroll's attitude toward the United States and the position Catholics should have in it was stated clearly in a message sent to George Washington in 1789 congratulating him on his election as president. Signed by Carroll "in behalf of the Roman Catholic Clergy" and by Charles Carroll, Daniel Carroll, and several others "in behalf of the Roman Catholic Laity", the message addressed these respectful but forceful words to Washington:

> You encourage respect for religion, and inculcate, by words and actions, that principle, on which the welfare of nations so much depends, that a superintending providence governs the events of the world.... This prospect of national prosperity is peculiarly pleasing to us on another account; because whilst our country preserves her freedom and independence, we shall have a well founded title to claim from her justice equal rights of citizenship, as the price of our blood spilt under your eyes, and of our common exertions for her defence.... We pray for the preservation of them, where they have been granted; and expect the full extension of them from the justice of those States, which still restrict them.[3]

Washington replied warmly in March of the following year. After thanking Carroll and his companions for their congratulations, he added: "I presume that your fellow-citizens will not forget the patriotic part which you took in the accomplishment of their Revolution, and the establishment of their government; or the important assistance which they received from a nation [France] in which the

---

[3] "The Catholics' Congratulations to President Washington, 1789, and His Reply, March 12, 1790", in *Documents of American Catholic History*, ed. John Tracy Ellis (Milwaukee: Bruce Publishing, 1962), 170–72.

Roman Catholic religion is professed." Washington closed by wishing the Catholics of the United States "every temporal and spiritual felicity".[4]

Later in 1790, taking possession of his diocese, Bishop Carroll lamented that it would no longer do for him to be merely "inoffensive in my conduct and regular in my manners". Instead, he observed, the duties of his office now included not only caring for the faithful of his vast see, with "nothing in view but God and your salvation", but also fostering "charity and forebearance [sic]" toward non-Catholic churches while at the same time not falling into the "fatal and prevailing indifference which views all religions as equally acceptable to God and salutary to men".

In essence, that remained his program for the next quarter century, and he was remarkably successful in carrying it out. At the time of his death, the Catholic Church in the United States was growing in numbers (close to 120,000), putting down institutional roots, and at peace with Protestant America. What neither John Carroll nor anyone else knew then or could have been expected to know was that America in 1815 stood poised on the brink of a vast influx of immigrants. Many of them were to be Catholics who would bring to the Church in America and the American nation both explosive expansion and an array of vexing new tensions and problems.

[4] Ibid.

SAINT ELIZABETH ANN SETON
(1774–1821)

"Love Says Let It Be"

An American woman, a pious Episcopalian from New York, was attending Mass with the Catholic friends with whom she was staying in Italy. As the ceremony progressed, she was deeply offended by the boorishness of a British tourist who shared with her *sotto voce* his contempt for the Italian congregation's visible faith in Christ's Real Presence in the consecrated Host that the priest held aloft.

Angry though the woman was, the incident got her thinking. "What *did* Catholics believe about the Eucharist? What made them believe it? And was there any possibility that they were right?" After hearing the Englishman's words whispered in her ear, she later wrote, "I bent from him to the pavement, and thought secretly on the word of St. Paul, with starting tears, 'They discern not the Lord's Body'; and the next thought was how should they eat and drink their very damnation for not *discerning* it, if indeed it is not *there*? Yet how should it be *there*? And how did *He* breathe my soul in me? And how, and how a hundred other things I know nothing about?"[1]

[1] Biographical information about Mother Seton is drawn largely from Joseph I. Dirvin, C.M., *Mrs. Seton: Foundress of the American Sisters of Charity* (New York: Farrar, Straus and Giroux, 1975). Unless otherwise noted, quotations from Mother Seton are taken from this source.

The American woman's name was Elizabeth Ann Seton. She didn't know it then, but a year later she was to become a Catholic herself. And although neither she nor anyone else dreamed such a thing, she was destined to become American Catholicism's first native-born canonized saint as well as the founder of the first religious community to be established in the United States and of the Catholic school system in America.

She also was something else. "Elizabeth Ann Seton was wholly American," Pope Paul VI exclaimed as he declared her a saint in 1975. "Splendid proof," he added, that America, too, is "fertile ground" for sanctity.[2]

She was born August 28, 1774, the second daughter of socially prominent parents in New York. Dr. Richard Bayley, her father, was the first professor of anatomy at Columbia College and chief health officer of the Port of New York. Her mother, Catherine Bayley, was the daughter of the rector of St. Andrew's Episcopal Church on Staten Island. Catherine died when Betty was three years old, and her father married Charlotte Barclay. They had seven children, including one whose son, James Roosevelt Bayley, converted to Catholicism, became the first bishop of Newark, and was eventually named seventh archbishop of Baltimore.

Raised an Episcopalian, Elizabeth had a normal child's interest in games and parties, but at an early age she also displayed a strong interest in religious matters. During a morning walk in the woods in May 1789, she experienced a sudden awareness that "God was my Father, my all." She wrote: "I prayed, sang hymns, cried, laughed, talking to myself of how far He could place me above all sorrow.

[2]Pope Paul VI, "Homily for the Canonization of Elisabeth Ann Seton", September 14, 1975, https://w2.vatican.va/content/paul-vi/en/homilies/1975/documents/hf_p-vi_hom_19750914.html.

Then I laid still to enjoy the heavenly peace that came over my soul; and I am sure, in the two hours so enjoyed, grew ten years in the spiritual life."

In January 1794 she married William Magee Seton, heir to a family export-import firm in New York. In time the happy couple had five children. Although her religious views in those days were, in the words of her biographer, Father Joseph Dirvin, C.M., a "hodgepodge of belief and observance", she remained deeply religious. She also counted herself blessed in her sister-in-law, Rebecca Seton, whom she considered the "friend of her soul". Eager to do good works, the two women became known as the "Protestant Sisters of Charity" for their assistance to the needy. (It should be noted that this was at a time when one of the curiosities on display in a New York wax museum was the effigy of a nun.)

Will Seton's father died in 1798, and Elizabeth cheerfully took on the responsibility of being a kind of substitute mother to her husband's younger siblings, while Will assumed both the family business and its financial difficulties, mounting due to causes that included piracy on the high seas. The final blow was the sinking of one of its merchant ships, with the loss of its valuable cargo. The export-import firm went bankrupt. Will Seton was ruined at the very time his health was failing from tuberculosis. The doctors believed the climate of Italy might help, and in October 1803 the Setons and their eight-year-old daughter, Anna, set out on a journey to visit Will's business associates and friends, the Filicchis, in the Italian port city of Livorno.

After a long voyage of seven weeks, they found more trouble awaiting them in Livorno. The port authorities quarantined Will because he came from New York, where yellow fever was then raging. The Setons were confined to damp, cold quarters, and the young husband and father grew steadily worse. On December 27 he died at the age of thirty-five.

At this desperate juncture, the Filicchis stepped in with an act of extraordinary generosity, insisting that the young widow and her daughter stay with them while recovering from the shock. It was at this time that the incident at Mass described above occurred.

Elizabeth and Anna sailed back to New York in the spring of 1804. But where the Filicchis had received her graciously, Elizabeth's reception by family and friends was anything but gracious, especially when they learned of her new interest in Catholicism. Adding to her sorrow was the premature death of her sister-in-law, Rebecca. Among her spiritual advisors in this time of troubles was Father John Cheverus, later to be the first Catholic bishop of Boston and after that cardinal archbishop of Bordeaux. Certain now what God wanted of her, Elizabeth Seton was received into the Catholic Church at St. Peter's parish in lower Manhattan on March 14, 1805. On Pentecost Sunday the following year, Bishop (later, Archbishop) John Carroll of Baltimore confirmed her.

One immediate result of her conversion, an especially painful one, was her virtual ostracism by the elders of the Seton family together with their refusal of financial assistance to her and her children. Needing to support herself and them, Elizabeth tried teaching at a Protestant couple's school, but the school soon failed. Then she tried running a boarding establishment for boys attending an Episcopalian minister's school, but she had to give that up when angry parents withdrew their sons. In a letter to her Italian friend Antonio Filicchi, she said, "In short, Tonino, they do not know what to do with me, *but God does*, and when his blessed time is come, we shall know."

In 1806 Father Louis William Dubourg, S.S., was visiting New York, and Elizabeth happened to meet him. Father Dubourg, one of a group of French Sulpician priests in Baltimore, president of St. Mary's College there, and later to be bishop of a French diocese, had the idea of creating a women's religious institute in America, modeled on the Daughters of Charity of St. Vincent de Paul. Elizabeth Seton impressed him as a likely candidate for the task.

In 1808 she moved to Baltimore and opened a school while also organizing other women who began to arrive into the nucleus of a religious community. On March 25, 1809, in the lower chapel of St. Mary's Seminary on Paca Street, she pronounced one-year vows of chastity and obedience to Archbishop Carroll, who gave her the title "Mother". "I shall be the mother of many daughters," she said. The following June, she and the other sisters appeared together in public wearing the costume worn by Italian widows of that day—black dresses and capes and white bonnets trimmed in black.

Mother Seton, her children, and her new sisters in religion now moved to Emmitsburg in rural Frederick County, Maryland, where a wealthy convert and seminarian named Samuel Cooper had donated a 269-acre site amid the rolling foothills as the location for a girls' school and other benevolent uses. The sisters called the site, near the recently founded Mount St. Mary's College and Seminary, St. Joseph's Valley. The Sisters of Charity of St. Joseph's settled in a former farmhouse and opened St. Joseph's Free School and St. Joseph's Academy in 1810.

The establishment of these two tiny institutions, the free school and the academy, is now commemorated as the birth of the parochial school system in the United States. To Antonio Filicchi's brother Filippo, the foundress wrote:

"I have invariably kept in the background and avoided even reflecting voluntarily on anything of the kind, knowing that Almighty God alone could effect it if indeed it will be realized. Father Mr. Dubourg has always said the same, be quiet, God will in his own time discover His intentions, nor will I allow one word of intreaty [sic] from my pen. His blessed will be done."[3]

Life in this isolated rural setting was by no means easy, and the new religious community suffered unavoidable growing pains. "I am a mother encompassed by many children, not all equally amiable or congenial," Mother Seton recorded. And another time, with her customary openness to God's will at work even in the distressing events of her life, she wrote: "Here I stand with hands and eyes both lifted to wait the Adorable Will. The only word I have to say to every question is: *I am a mother.* Whatever providence awaits me consistent with that plea, I say Amen to it."

But the Sisters of Charity took root and grew. Close to seventy of the first ninety-eight candidates not only opted to join the community but remained members for life. Soon new foundations were being launched. In 1814 the sisters opened the first Catholic orphanage in the United States—St. Joseph's Asylum in Philadelphia. By 1830 they were operating orphanages and schools as far west as Cincinnati and New Orleans, and in St. Louis they had established the first hospital west of the Mississippi. In 1850, the American community formally merged with the French Daughters of Charity, as Mother Seton had intended. Of the five Seton children, two became religious sisters themselves—Anna Maria, who took her vows

---

[3] "Mother Seton's Plans for Her Religious Community, February 9, 1809", in *Documents of American Catholic History*, ed. John Tracy Ellis (Milwaukee: Bruce Publishing, 1962), 189.

as a member of her mother's community on her deathbed, and Catherine, who was a founding member of the Sisters of Mercy in New York and spent more than forty years engaged in prison ministry there.

Mother Seton died of tuberculosis on January 4, 1821. She was forty-six. James Cardinal Gibbons of Baltimore began the cause for her canonization in 1882. Pope Saint John XXIII beatified her—declared her "blessed"—on March 17, 1963. Her canonization by Pope Paul VI took place on September 14, 1975. In proclaiming her a saint, he cited her as an example of "what women can and must accomplish in the fulfillment of their role for the good of humanity".[4]

Today the parochial school system in the United States, one of the most remarkable institutional achievements of American Catholicism, stands as a monument to her life and work. But the system has been in steep numerical decline for the last half century and continues to decline at the time this is written.

According to the National Catholic Educational Association, Catholic elementary and secondary school enrollment in the United States reached its peak in the early 1960s, when there were more than 5.2 million students in over thirteen thousand schools nationwide. The 2014–2015 enrollment figure was 1,939,574—1,359,969 in elementary and middle schools; 579,605 in secondary schools—with 20.4 percent of the students racial minorities, 15.3 percent Hispanic/Latino, and 6.3 percent unknown. Non-Catholics were 16.9 percent of the total. Catholic schools numbered 6,568 (5,368 elementary; 1,200 secondary). Where a half century ago religious, especially religious sisters, were by far the largest part of the Catholic

[4] Paul VI, "Homily for the Canonization of Elisabeth Ann Seton".

schools' teaching staff, by 2014–2015 laypeople, predominantly women, made up 97.2 percent of the staff.[5]

Several reasons account for this decline. These include rising costs and the continued denial of significant government assistance to these institutions despite the important services they render to communities across the country, a falling birth rate, and the absence of Catholic schools in many places. In the estimate of many people, however, something else may also be part of the mix—a weakened commitment to the faith on the part of not a few Catholic parents who in earlier times might have sent their children to Catholic schools but today see no compelling reason for doing that, given the availability of free public schools or, in the case of the affluent and socially ambitious among them, high-cost, high-prestige private institutions.

Whatever the reason or combination of reasons, it seems likely that Mother Seton would have seen God's will at work even in this dismaying situation. To the "friend of her soul", Rebecca Seton, she summed up her view of life in these words: "Faith lifts the staggering soul on one side, hope supports it on the other, experience says it must be, and love says let it be."

[5] National Catholic Educational Association, Public Policy and Data, "United States Catholic Elementary and Secondary Schools 2014–2015: The Annual Statistical Report on Schools, Enrollment, and Staffing", accessed February 8, 2015, https://www.ncea.org/data-information/catholic-school-data.

ARCHBISHOP JOHN HUGHES
(1797–1864)

"Become Merged in the Country of Your Adoption"

How typical of John Hughes—still getting people mad at him fifteen years after his death. This time the issue was St. Patrick's Cathedral, today perhaps the best-known Catholic house of worship in the United States but then a tempting target for anti-Catholic venom. New York's cathedral was dedicated in a splendid, hours-long ceremony on the morning of Sunday, May 25, 1879. Shortly before the event, the *Atlantic Monthly*, a mouthpiece of the Northeast's non-Catholic establishment, ran an article trashing the building and Archbishop Hughes, whose great project it was. He'd been dead since 1864.

The author, an architectural critic named Clarence Cook, wrote that the fourth bishop of New York was a "politician" as well as a priest—one of the few Catholic priests "able to win, by their own character and energy, a national reputation". "We are not saying it was an agreeable reputation," Cook continued. "The archbishop belonged to the church militant ... always in the saddle, never weary, and, what was more never desponding ... so convincing that, when he called for money, if a

29

widow had but one penny, yet should he have a farthing ere he went."[1]

Someone reading that now may wonder what lay behind this bilious outburst against a long-dead prelate. Historian Charles R. Morris offers this explanation: Cook grasped the symbolism of St. Patrick's just as Archbishop Hughes had done; but where the archbishop had cherished it, Cook, to say the least, did not. "It enunciated a vision of Catholicism as a new power center, a major moral and political force," Morris writes. "Cook was shouting, Beware! With a man of John Hughes's forcefulness at the head of the Catholic Church in the United States, anything *could* happen." And Hughes? It seems likely that he would have replied in kind to Cook's attack—and then much enjoyed the verbal fisticuffs that followed.

John Hughes reigned—the word suits the reality—as archbishop of New York from December 1842 until his death in January 1864. In those two decades he established himself in the eyes of fellow Americans as a Catholic bishop unlike any they'd seen till then. Archbishop John Carroll of Baltimore and his successors tended to be cautious, low-profile prelates who worked hard to avoid upsetting the non-Catholic society in which American Catholics desired to win acceptance. Hughes was something else—high-profile, combative, aggressive, never shrinking from, and actually seeming to relish, a really good fight.

While personality differences between the archbishop of New York and others in the American hierarchy obviously had much to do with that, so did numbers. When

---

[1] Quoted in Charles R. Morris, *American Catholic* (New York: Times Books, 1997). Biographical information about Archbishop Hughes is drawn largely from this source as are the quotations from Archbishop Hughes, unless otherwise noted.

Archbishop Carroll died in 1815, Catholics in the United States totaled only 120,000. But between 1820 and 1870, 2.7 million Catholic immigrants poured into the country. Most came from Germany, France, and Ireland—especially Ireland. From his vantage point in New York, Archbishop Hughes presided over the peak years of that influx.

Clearly, the times were changing then, and so was the Catholic presence in America. Hughes embodied the change and did his vigorous best to turn it to the advantage of the Church and the nation alike. He was, says Morris, the "archetype" of a "new breed" of bishop who "imposed order and discipline on fractious urban dioceses and started building the vast network of Catholic institutions" that has continued to be a notable feature of American Catholicism up to the present.

At the beginning, no one would have guessed all that. John Joseph Hughes was born June 24, 1797, in the southern part of Ireland's County Tyrone, third of seven children of a hardworking tenant farmer. The young man came to the United States in 1817. Drawn to the priesthood, he soon applied for admission to Mount St. Mary's Seminary in Emmitsburg, Maryland, but he was turned down for being academically unprepared and was hired as a gardener instead. Around this time, he met Mother Elizabeth Seton, convert foundress of the Daughters of Charity in the United States, and through the intercession of this future saint was admitted to the seminary as a student by its French rector, Father Jean Dubois. Ordained in 1826, he took up pastoral work in the Archdiocese of Philadelphia, where he earned a measure of fame in a public controversy with a Presbyterian minister who had attacked the Church.

In 1837, John Hughes was named coadjutor bishop of New York at the request of its ordinary—his former seminary rector, Jean Dubois. Consecrated in January 1838, the hard-driving coadjutor quickly took charge of the diocese's affairs from the elderly Dubois, whom he succeeded in December 1842. In 1850 New York was elevated to the status of an archdiocese, and Hughes received the title archbishop.

The challenges facing him were many. Besides the pressing need to respond to the immigration-fueled explosion of Catholic numbers, Archbishop Hughes, along with his fellow American bishops, confronted a rising tide of anti-Catholicism that accompanied this Catholic expansion. In 1834, an Ursuline convent in Charlestown, Massachusetts, outside Boston, had been burned to the ground by a mob whose members imagined they were rescuing a woman imprisoned there against her will. The incident signaled the start of two decades of violence aimed at immigrants and Catholics. Two years after the burning of the convent, a mob burned most of the Irish section of Boston. Violence flared in Philadelphia, and churches, convents, and Irish homes burned there, too. Clashes between Catholics and non-Catholics occurred repeatedly in many American cities through the 1840s.

There was trouble in New York as well. "Are you afraid?" the city's mayor taunted the archbishop. "Yes," was the answer. "Not for my churches but for yours. If a single Catholic church is burned here, New York will be turned into another Moscow." Then he ringed his parish churches with armed Irishmen. No Catholic churches or convents burned in New York.

Archbishop Hughes ran the archdiocese's internal affairs with a similarly strong hand—so strong, in fact, that his priests took to calling him "Dagger John". The nickname referred to the cross he placed before his signature on documents—and also to his pugnacious manner. "I will suffer no man in my diocese that I cannot control," he is said to have snapped during a run-in with the Catholic convert writer and social thinker Orestes Brownson, himself no slouch as a controversialist. Brownson took the hint and moved his base of operations across the Hudson to New Jersey.

But Hughes was more than just a petty tyrant. He was a successful administrator, a builder of churches, promoter of parochial schools, champion of the Irish, skilled manipulator of the levers of politics, and along with everything else, a patriot of multiple loyalties: loyal to Ireland, loyal to his Irish immigrants, loyal to the United States, but above all loyal to his Church. "Never forget your country," he lectured his faithful. By "country" he meant Ireland, and the Catholics he was addressing were Irish-born like himself. But then he went on: "Let this love of old Ireland affect you only individually. In your social and political relations you must become merged in the country of your adoption."

The archbishop was under no illusions about the wretched conditions of the Irish poor in many large Eastern cities. "There are," he agreed, "great numbers of Irish emigrants who have to struggle against all the miseries incident to their condition," and these unhappy souls would only be further "deteriorated physically, religiously, or morally" by being dumped out West to take up farming, as various schemes—cockeyed in Hughes' unsentimental view—would have it. On the whole, he believed, the Irish were better off staying where they were—in the big cities—and working to better themselves by bootstrap methods as some wealthy Irish had already done through their exercise of "industry and enterprise".[2] In this way, whether deliberately or not, he was helping set the stage

[2]"Archbishop Hughes' Opposition to Western Civilization for Catholic Immigrants", in *Documents of American Catholic History*, ed. John Tracy Ellis (Milwaukee: Bruce Publishing, 1962), 317–21.

for the emergence of Irish political power via the Irish-dominated political machines that soon appeared in cities like New York, Boston, and Chicago.

As with the Irish, so also with the United States, Archbishop Hughes saw many faults and failings but even so loved America deeply. In a long report to Rome concerning conditions in America, written in 1858, he sought to disabuse the Holy See of the notion that liberty in America meant what it meant in the Old World. "In Continental Europe," he wrote, "liberty is understood to mean the overthrow of all existing governments recognizing the principle of Monarchy. It is the genius of destruction and bloodshed:—ferociously bent on pulling down whatever exists, without the fore-sight or capacity to substitute any thing as good or better."

And the United States? "Liberty, in this Country … means the vindication of personal rights; the fair support of public laws; the maintenance, at all hazards, of public order, according to those laws; the right to change them when they are found to be absurd or oppressive." And the "excesses"—such as mob action and lynchings—that marred the American scene? "I can assure you that these excesses are regarded, here, as outrages and violations of liberty, the same as they would be in Europe."[3]

His devotion to the United States found patriotic expression just a few years later at a crucial moment in the Civil War. Hughes and William H. Seward had become good friends during Seward's years as governor of New York. In October 1861 Seward, now Abraham Lincoln's secretary of state, turned to the archbishop with an unusual request: travel to Europe as an unofficial representative of

[3] "Archbishop Hughes Interprets American Liberty and Its Abuses to the Holy See", *Documents*, 329–35.

the U.S. government and attempt to persuade Catholic powers France and Spain to remain neutral in the American conflict.

Hughes accepted the assignment and on January 27, 1862, wrote Seward from Paris reporting notable success. Having spent much time in France attending receptions and dinner parties at which he unabashedly advocated the Union cause, he was at last granted an audience with the emperor Napoleon III and the empress Eugenie during which he did the same. Now, he was pleased to tell his old friend, Napoleon III had delivered a speech to the French legislative assembly just two days earlier in which, while acknowledging the injury to the French textile industry in being cut off from Southern cotton by the Union's blockade of the Confederacy, the emperor nevertheless concluded that France should stay out of the conflict.

"All that, under present circumstances, we could have hoped for," Hughes crowed to Seward, adding—not too modestly—"I have done all I could to bring about the result." (As for Spain, on a trip to Rome he delivered the same message to the Spanish ambassador and two Spanish cardinals.) In closing, the archbishop took the occasion to tell Seward—no doubt hoping and expecting it would reach the president's ears—that in France Lincoln was "winning golden opinions for his calm, unostentatious, mild, but firm and energetic administrative talents".[4]

As Clarence Cook's attack on him long after his death suggests, Archbishop Hughes had more than his share of enemies, some of whom he may have earned. But some of the enemies weren't above fictionalizing to damage his reputation. That was the case with an urban legend

---

[4]"The Efforts of Archbishop Hughes to Keep France Neutral During the Civil War", *Documents*, 370–73.

concerning the acquisition of the land on which St. Patrick's Cathedral was built. According to this version of events—repeated by Cook—the devious archbishop had pulled strings to obtain a sweetheart deal that allowed him to buy the site "for the consideration of one dollar".

This was malicious fantasy. The city had sold the land to a private party in 1799, and the property had several owners in succession before the future cathedral's trustees acquired the title in 1852 for $59,500—a significant sum back then. Yet even some modern histories of New York repeat the tale of the Hughes-engineered sweetheart deal that never was.

In the end, of course, the city's Irish and their archbishop were vindicated. Today St. Patrick's Cathedral stands in the heart of midtown Manhattan as a monument to faith, vision, and determination. *The Catholics have arrived*, the mighty Church still proclaims, *and Archbishop John Hughes had—still has, in fact—quite a bit to do with that.*

ORESTES BROWNSON
(1803–1876)

An American Ultramontanist

Death can be as full of surprises as life itself. By the time he died, Orestes Brownson, the most distinguished American Catholic public intellectual of the nineteenth century, had become a ferocious critic of the Americanist path taken by most of his fellow American Catholics. Yet by one of life's quirks, Brownson lies buried today in the crypt of the campus church at Notre Dame University, the flagship institution of American Catholicism's impulse to Americanize.

For all anyone knows, of course, the volatile Brownson might have been pleased at that. But a reaction of a very different sort is suggested by his acid observation that there's "scarcely a trait in the American character ... that is not more or less hostile to Catholicity".[1]

Brownson was a difficult man—"one of the most rugged and forceful of personalities", historian Theodore Maynard called him. But together with his fighting spirit, he combined a powerful intellect that made him more than a polemicist—a thinker to be reckoned with. Brownson's book *The American Republic*, published shortly after the

[1] Brownson is the subject of many studies. Biographical details for this sketch are drawn largely from Patrick W. Carey, *Orestes A. Brownson: American Religious Weathervane* (Grand Rapids, Mich.: William B. Eerdmans, 2004). Unless otherwise indicated, quotations are from this source.

Civil War, is still read and discussed as a significant contribution to American political philosophy. Today, too, his mordant analysis of the impact of Americanism on the faith of American Catholics merits serious attention.

Orestes Augustus Brownson was born September 16, 1803, in Stockbridge, Vermont. His father died when he was two, and he was raised by a nonpracticing Congregationalist couple. Although receiving little formal schooling, he read furiously, self-educating himself in the ideas and intellectual trends of the day, especially those with a bearing on religion. First he became a Presbyterian, then a Unitarian minister, then a minister of the Congregationalist church, then for a short time minister of his own Boston-based "Church of the Future".

In Boston he came into contact with Transcendentalism —the post-Christian quasi-religious movement that attracted such members of the New England intellectual elite as Ralph Waldo Emerson, Bronson Alcott, and Margaret Fuller. Brownson was drawn to them at first but soon went his own way. In an essay on Emerson years later, he said of the Transcendentalists:

> Falling into a sort of transcendental illuminism, [they] sank into pure naturalism.... There was much life, mental activity, and honest purpose in the movement; but those who had the most influence in directing its course could not believe that anything good could come out of Nazareth, and so turned their backs on the Church. They thought they could find something deeper, broader, and more living than Christianity, and have lost not only the transient but even the permanent in religion.[2]

[2] Orestes Augustus Brownson, "Emerson's Prose Works", in *The Brownson Reader*, ed. Alvan S. Ryan (New York: P.J. Kenedy and Sons, 1955), 182. The essay was originally published in 1870.

In 1837 he launched a journal called *Brownson's Quarterly Review*, as a platform for his social, political, economic, literary, and religious views. Combined with his frequent lecturing, the *Review* made him a national figure in a few years.

In 1841 or 1842 Brownson had a profound religious experience that opened his eyes to the reality of God as a benign father. Continuing his religious search, he drew ever closer to Catholicism, and on October 20, 1844, was received into the Church. In *The Convert*, an 1857 volume describing his religious journey, he explained: "As the Roman Catholic Church is clearly the church of history, the only church that can have the slightest historical claim to be regarded as the Body of Christ, it is to her I must go, and her teachings, as given through her pastors, that I must accept as authoritative for natural reason. It was, no doubt, unpleasant to take such a step, but to be eternally damned would, after all, be a great deal unpleasanter."

A few years later, satirizing Brownson's well-known changeability in a verse that also spoke of Emerson and Alcott, poet James Russell Lowell wrote of him:

> He shifts quite about, then proceeds to expound
> That 'tis merely the earth, not himself, that turns
>   round,
> And wishes it clearly impressed on your mind
> That the weathercock rules and not follows the
>   wind.

Although that assessment contained more than a little truth, Orestes Brownson was nonetheless a man of stature in the busy intellectual world of his day. So much so that when the eminent British convert and scholar John Henry Newman was preparing to launch a Catholic university in

Dublin, the American "weathercock" was the first person whom he invited to join the faculty. Brownson was flattered and attracted by the offer. But the Irish bishops vetoed the appointment of a man who even then had a transatlantic reputation for holding sometimes controversial views. Newman was obliged to suggest that he not visit Ireland just then. Seeing how things stood, Brownson said no thanks to the job offer.

His outspoken and polemical manner similarly made the distinguished convert an embarrassment to American bishops who preferred a less in-your-face approach. Nor did he make many friends by broadcasting his distaste for the Irish Americans who'd become a dominant presence in American Catholicism and whom Brownson in *The Convert* provocatively dismissed as "nominally Catholic".

His most famous tussle with a member of the hierarchy involved Archbishop John Hughes, the feisty Irish American who headed the Archdiocese of New York from 1842 to 1864. Brownson moved to New York in 1845 at Archbishop Hughes' invitation, and there resumed publication of his journal, now called *Brownson's Review*. But the combative editor and the no less combative churchman soon fell out over issues of style and substance. In consequence, the editor took the prudent step of moving himself and his *Review* to the less stressful atmosphere of Elizabeth, New Jersey.

A sharp, not to say bitter, critic of his fellow Catholics, Brownson in an 1861 essay claimed to know of "no epoch in which the directors of the Catholic world seem to have had so great a dread of intellect as our own.... There is a widespread fear that he who thinks will think heretically." This was shortsighted policy, Brownson declared, at a time when religion could expect no protection from the state against dissension and disbelief. The conclusion was obvious: "The faithful must be guarded and protected by being trained and disciplined to grapple with the errors and false systems of the age. They must be not only more religiously, but also more intellectually educated."[3]

As time passed, he grew increasingly conservative, though hardly less controversial, in his religious opinions, aligning himself with Ultramontanism—the school that placed heavy emphasis on the authority of the pope. During and after the First Vatican Council (1869–1870), he strongly supported the definition of the dogmas of papal infallibility and papal primacy. With the Vatican and the Italian nationalist movement locked in a struggle that ended with the pope's loss of the Papal States, Brownson wrote in support of the temporal authority of the papacy, including even the pope's power to depose secular rulers. And as secular opinion in Europe turned increasingly against the Church, the American Ultramontanist saw the same thing happening in the United States while his American coreligionists dozed. "Even our Republic goes the way of all the earth," he wrote angrily, "and our Catholic population hardly seem aware of their mission as Catholics. Outside of the Sanctuary they are hardly distinguishable in their social and political action from non-Catholics."

Brownson's long and sometimes contentious friendship with Father Isaac Hecker, the founder of the Paulist Fathers, has with good reason been called one of the great stories of American Catholic history, for it sheds important light on the central issue in the Catholic experience in the United States—the Americanization of Catholics and their Church.

The two men had been close since the early 1840s, and Brownson was instrumental in Hecker's conversion to

---

[3] "Catholic Polemics", in Ryan, *Brownson Reader*, 334, 336.

Catholicism even though his young friend actually preceded him into the Church by a few months. For a long time, they shared the conviction that America was ripe for conversion, a theme expounded by Father Hecker in several books and in his magazine the *Catholic World*, for which Brownson often wrote.

In his masterpiece, *The American Republic*, Brownson took an elevated view of the United States, writing that it had been given a "mission from God".

> Its idea is ... liberty with law, and law with liberty. Yet its mission is not so much the realization of liberty as the realization of the true idea of the state, which secures at once the authority of the public and the freedom of the individual.... In other words, its mission is to bring out in its life the dialectic union of authority and liberty, of the natural rights of man and those of society.... The American republic has been instituted by Providence to realize the freedom of each with advantage to the other.[4]

But Brownson's view of America darkened after the Civil War. Political disillusionment set in as he mourned the loss of two sons in the conflict, while his wife's health failed and his own health declined. An ardent advocate of the Union during the war, he had hoped for postwar reconciliation with the South and was disgusted by the vindictive policy pursued by Congress after Lincoln's death. Like other observers of the American scene such as Henry Adams—historian, author of a famous autobiography, and grandson and great-grandson of presidents—he came to believe that American democracy had suffered a deplorable falling-off since the glory days of the Revolutionary and immediate post-Revolutionary eras.

[4] From the *American Republic*, in Ryan, *Brownson Reader*, 70–71.

Brownson's critique also had a distinctively Catholic dimension, which he had expressed earlier in his review of a book by Isaac Hecker. Here Brownson rejected the notion that evangelizing America would be an easy task. The American people as a whole, he wrote, were "imbued with a spirit of independence, an aversion to authority, a pride, an overwhelming conceit, as well as with a prejudice that makes them revolt at the bare mention of the Church".

By 1870 the split between the two men was irreparable. In a letter written from Rome during Vatican Council I, Father Hecker spoke of the admiration he'd encountered among Europeans for the friendly relations existing between Catholicism and "our free institutions" in the United States. Brownson's reply was withering. Where he had once discerned a God-given mission for the United States, he declared that he now accepted the American system merely as "the legal & only practicable form" for the country, adding: "I no longer hope anything of it." As for the prospects that Catholics would convert America, he said: "So far are we from converting the country, we cannot hold our own." Citing an American spirit of "independence, freedom from all restraint, unbounded license" that he believed was infecting Catholics, Brownson wrote: "The Church has never encountered a social & political order so hostile to her ... the conversion of our republic will be a far greater victory than the conversion of the Roman Empire."[6]

Their friendship survived the shock, but by now the two had moved far apart on many matters, and Brownson

[6] The exchange of letters can be found in Joseph F. Gower and Richard M. Leliaert, eds., *The Brownson-Hecker Correspondence* (Notre Dame, Ind.: University of Notre Dame Press, 1979), 278–93.

soon stopped writing for the *Catholic World*. Before he did, though, at Hecker's request he penned an essay on church and state in which he declared his verdict on the nation: "The American democracy is not what it was in 1776. It was then Christian after a Protestant fashion; it is now infected with European liberalism, or popular absolutism; and if we had to introduce the American system now, we should not be able to do it." As for America's Catholics, in a passage that today seems almost eerily far-sighted in light of current events, he wrote: "We shall find even Catholics who ... gravely tell us that their religion has nothing to do with their politics; that is, their politics are independent of their religion; that is, again, politics are independent of God, and there is no God in the political order; as if a man could be an atheist in the state, and devout Catholic in the church."

Having moved to Detroit to be with his son Henry, Brownson lived on until 1876, becoming ever more testy as the years passed. After a rousing theological argument with Henry on Good Friday, he took to his bed, received the last sacraments, and died on Easter Monday, April 17. He was buried in Detroit. Ten years later, his remains were transferred to Notre Dame.

Orestes Brownson left neither disciples nor an integrated body of work. He was an intellectual bomb thrower, a volcano of provocative insights who often and without apology changed his mind—though never his loyalty to the Catholic faith he had embraced. But with all his failings and limitations, he occupies a lasting place in America's intellectual history and in the history of the Church, where he had at last found the truth. "I owe much ... to your father," Isaac Hecker told Brownson's son. Others might say the same.

FATHER ISAAC HECKER
(1819–1888)

"God's Providence Was Preparing Me for a Great Work"

In late spring or early summer of 1842, Isaac Hecker had a vision. Standing next to him was "a beautiful angelic pure being" whose presence caused him to feel "a most heavenly pure joy".[1] It was a life-changing experience that set the young man, just twenty-two at the time, in search of a way of life that would correspond to it. And although there is no record that Hecker had any more visions after that, in a larger sense the founder of the Paulist Fathers remained a visionary for as long as he lived.

His great goal was the conversion of Protestant America to Catholicism, and he was convinced that it was realizable. After all, he insisted, in the United States "true religion will find a reception it has in vain looked for elsewhere." If ever Isaac Hecker is declared a saint (the process that could have that result began in 2008, and he now has the title "Servant of God"), it's this conviction that Catholicism had found its providential home in America that moves one to imagine him being designated patron

[1] Biographical information about Hecker is drawn largely from David J. O'Brien, *Isaac Hecker: An American Catholic* (New York: Paulist Press, 1992). Unless otherwise indicated, quotations are from this source.

of the Americanist impulse in American Catholicism. In the realm of ideas, surely, no one before or since has done more than Hecker to encourage Catholic assimilation into the secular culture of the United States.

He was born December 18, 1819, in New York, third son and youngest child of a German American immigrant family. The Heckers were bakers, a trade Isaac also pursued. Although having few if any ties with a church, from early on he exhibited an uncommon interest in religion. In time, that interest led him to the vaguely religious movement of New England intellectuals called Transcendentalism and to the experimental communities at Brook Farm and Fruitland. Traveling in these heady circles, the young man was at first influenced by Ralph Waldo Emerson, the most prominent American thinker of the early nineteenth century, of whom Hecker's friend and mentor Orestes Brownson was to write that he came "as near to the truth as one can who is so unhappy as to miss it". Eventually, however, Hecker soured on Emerson, complaining that the great man had "no conception of church".

It was around this time that he met and became friends with Brownson, who by then was already a well-known writer and lecturer on religious and social questions and like Hecker a religious seeker. Brownson, sixteen years his senior, pointed his young friend in the direction of Catholicism. As early as April 1843 Hecker wrote in his diary, "The Catholic Church alone seems to satisfy my wants." On August 1, 1844, he was baptized by Bishop (later, Cardinal) John McCloskey of New York. Brownson entered the Church soon after.

Feeling himself called to the priesthood, Hecker joined the Redemptorist order and, after seminary studies in Belgium, was ordained in October 1849 by Nicholas Cardinal Wiseman of Westminster. Returning to the United States,

Father Hecker took up the ministry of a Redemptorist missionary. At the same time, as his vision of a Catholic America grew and took shape, he also began setting down his ideas on paper. The result, a book called *Questions of the Soul*, was published in 1855. It was widely discussed and earned its author a national reputation.

Overt anti-Catholicism was by now an ugly reality in sectors of American society. As Protestants reacted with alarm to the influx of Irish and German immigrants, riots and church burnings had erupted in Philadelphia and other communities. A newly formed organization of Protestant ministers declared that its purpose was "to awaken the attention of the community to the dangers which threaten the liberties, and the public and domestic institutions, of these United States from the assaults of Romanism". In the early 1850s—around the time of Hecker's book, that is—the virulently anti-Catholic Know Nothing movement briefly became a potent force in national politics.

Nevertheless, where others saw a grave threat, Hecker, ever the visionary, saw opportunity. Arguing that Protestantism failed to meet the needs of seekers like himself, he wrote that the time was drawing near when the Catholic Church would be seen as the answer such people were looking for. Says biographer David O'Brien: "Hecker called for nothing less than a Catholic America, for the sake not of the church but of the nation and its people."

Two years later, moving quickly to take advantage of his first book's success, Father Hecker published *Aspirations of Nature*, a volume in which he spelled out his vision for evangelizing the United States and the logic of the nation's conversion to Catholicism. To his sorrow, *Aspirations* received far less attention than its predecessor had. Especially disappointing to its author was a review by Orestes Brownson in his own *Quarterly Review* pooh-poohing the idea that America was congenial ground for Catholic missionary work. The number of "earnest seekers" was, he maintained, far less than Hecker supposed, and in truth there was "scarcely a trait in the American character ... that is not more or less hostile to Catholicity".

Meanwhile Hecker was growing increasingly dissatisfied with the Redemptorists, whom he considered more interested in conducting parish missions for German Catholics transplanted to the United States than in converting intellectuals like his old Brook Farm friends. In August 1857 he made an unauthorized trip to Rome to argue his case with the order's head. But for his pains he was instead expelled from the order—or, in some versions, quit. Still, the trip was far from a dead loss. During his time in Rome the personable American met Pope Pius IX and won the pope's support for his ambitious scheme of evangelization. Back in the United States the following year, he and four other ex-Redemptorists came together to form a new religious order—the Congregation of the Missionary Priests of St. Paul the Apostle, better known as the Paulists—with Father Hecker as superior general.

A letter he sent to a friend in 1859 provides a revealing insight into Hecker's character as well as his ambitious aims. Earlier in his career, he writes, he was strongly attracted to "solitude, silence, prayer, contemplation", so much so that his religious superiors believed he might have a vocation to the contemplative life. At the time, though, another conviction grew upon him: "While most helpless and by others regarded as a fool, it was my most intimate conviction that God's Providence was preparing me for a great work, the conversion of our countrymen." The founding of the Paulists sprang from that.

The peculiarly American character of the new order was an essential part of it, Father Hecker explained.

"Individually the faith has been identified with American life. Our effort is to identify Catholicity with American life in a religious association. I feel confident of its practicability. I entertain the hope of our opening a door to our young men who aim at consecrating their lives to God & Religion, and of our Institution becoming in the hands of Divine Providence a means of spreading the Faith among our people."[2]

In the years that followed, Hecker was a very busy man. He traveled constantly, delivering lectures to largely non-Catholic audiences. On one trip alone he covered forty-five hundred miles and spoke to some thirty thousand people—a very considerable number in the days before radio, television, and social media. "He is putting American machinery into the old ark and is getting ready to run her by steam," one writer remarked. In 1865 he launched a magazine, the *Catholic World*, which was to continue in existence for over a century. The following year he founded a publishing house, Paulist Press, which is still in operation today.

During the First Vatican Council (1869–1870), Father Hecker wangled a place for himself on its fringes as a representative of the nonattending bishop of Columbus, Ohio. At first he agreed with the faction that considered it untimely for the council to adopt a formal definition of the doctrine of papal infallibility, but after Vatican I actually defined the dogma, he welcomed it and even saw it as a potential asset to the evangelization of America.

---

[2] "Father Hecker Sketches His Plans and Hopes for the Paulists, July 24, 1859", letter to Father Adrien-Emmanuel Rouquette, in *Documents of American Catholic History*, ed. John Tracy Ellis (Milwaukee: Bruce Publishing, 1962), 340–42. Rouquette was a writer and missionary with whom Hecker had begun a correspondence the year before in response to some friendly words about him published by Rouquette in the *Freeman's Journal* of New York.

Writing from Rome early in 1870, he sent his friend Brownson a remarkable letter that drew a no less remarkable response. The terms of the debate over the relationship of the Catholic Church to the American ethos have rarely been set out as starkly as they are in Hecker's missive and Brownson's reply.[3]

Hecker wrote with characteristic enthusiasm of the reception he'd received from Europeans who admired the American arrangement between church and state. Contemporary Europe, he believed, was in a transition from "a partial and temporary separation" between the two to some form of "more perfect union". In these circumstances, an article from Brownson for the *Catholic World* clearly setting out how things stood in the United States would be both timely and helpful. He explained: "In our own country, where the Church exists in her entire independance [*sic*] from State control, yet all her rights acknowledged and protected by the laws of the country, where her right to hold property, of establishing colleges, schools, charitable associations, etc. and to govern and administer her affairs according to her own laws and customs; it is here she is putting forth an energy and making conquests which vie with the zeal & success of the early ages of Christianity."

As we saw earlier, Brownson wasn't buying it. Although still accepting the American system as "the legal & only practicable form" for the nation as it was, he judged this system to be in fundamental conflict with Catholicism. "Catholics as well as others imbibe the spirit of the country ... freedom from all restraint, unbounded license. So far are we from converting the country, we cannot hold our

---

[3] See the exchange of letters in Joseph F. Gower and Richard M. Leliaert, eds., *The Brownson-Hecker Correspondence* (Notre Dame, Ind.: University of Notre Dame Press, 1979), 278–93.

own," Brownson exclaimed. The friendship between the two men survived the shock, but just barely.

Soon after Vatican I, Hecker's health went into decline. He lingered in Europe—by one account, he was suffering from leukemia and seeking a cure—then finally returned to the United States to pass his last years in a semi-invalid state while growing increasingly isolated within the community he'd founded. Worn out by illness and disappointed hopes, he died on December 21, 1888, after blessing the Paulists with whom he lived.

Inevitably, Isaac Hecker's name came to be linked to what is known as "Americanism". The story, a tangled one, is briefly this.

In 1896 a *Life of Isaac Thomas Hecker* by a Paulist named Walter Elliott was published in a French translation with a long introduction by a liberal French priest, Felix Klein, that made exaggerated claims for Hecker. By now, the Vatican was worried about trends in liberal Catholicism in Europe, especially France, that it associated with the Church in the United States and with the founder of the Paulists, and the Hecker biography with its provocative introduction only made things worse. In 1899 therefore Pope Leo XIII published a document addressed to the leader of the American hierarchy, James Cardinal Gibbons of Baltimore, in which the pope specifically condemned ideas that he lumped together under the heading "Americanism". To some people, Americanism sounded suspiciously like Isaac Hecker.[4]

Historians sympathetic to the Americanizing impulse in American Catholicism typically shrug off the papal critique

---

[4]See Pope Leo XIII, Letter *Testem Benevolentiae* to the Archbishop of Baltimore, in *Compendium of Creeds, Definitions, and Declarations on Matters of Faith and Morals*, ed. Heinrich Denziger, Peter Hünermann, Robert Fastiggi, and Anne Englund Nash (San Francisco: Ignatius Press, 2012), 3340–46.

and call Americanism a phantom heresy. Whatever the truth of the matter may have been just then, however, Pope Leo today appears as a man ahead of his time; for his 1899 document is a startlingly prescient warning against tendencies in vogue in progressive Catholic circles in America and elsewhere in the years since Vatican Council II (1962–1965), including disregard for the evangelical virtues, leading to "disregard for the religious life" and the pick-and-choose approach to Church teaching that often is described as cafeteria Catholicism.

If this way of thinking is to be believed, Pope Leo says, the Church needs to "relax its old severity" and take a more indulgent view of things, including even "the doctrines in which the deposit of faith is contained". Part of this involves a new version of "liberty" in the Church according to which "the faithful may indulge somewhat more freely each one his own mind." And ultimately: "The entire external teaching office is rejected [by those who say] that the Holy Spirit now pours forth into the souls of the faithful more and richer gifts than in times past, and, with no intermediary, by a kind of hidden instinct teaches and moves them."[5] It is only a short distance from this aberration to the exaggerated rhetoric sometimes heard today concerning the *sensus fidelium* as a criterion—perhaps *the* criterion—for settling questions of faith.

But how much does any of this have to do with Isaac Hecker? The driving force of his life was not a craving to erode the Catholic belief system but an ardent desire to spread it. "The conversion of the American people to the Catholic faith has ripened into a conviction with me which lies beyond the reign of doubt. My life, my labours,

---

[5] Ibid., 3342:676.

and my death [are] consecrated to it," he declared in the 1859 letter quoted above in which he sets forth his hopes and dreams for the religious order he had founded. Now as in his lifetime he is best understood as a visionary and an optimist who wanted Catholics to enter the American mainstream in order to convert it. If that hasn't happened just yet, it's hardly Hecker's fault.

FATHER MICHAEL McGIVNEY
(1852–1890)

"The Honor as Its Founder Will Be His"

In most ways, Father Michael J. McGivney appeared to be no more—and certainly no less—than another member of that largely unsung band of hardworking priests of immigrant stock who spent themselves building up the Church in America in the latter years of the nineteenth century. But in one remarkable respect he was unique: before he was thirty, McGivney had founded what was to become the largest Catholic men's organization in the world—the Knights of Columbus.

It happened, virtually unnoticed, in early February 1882 in New Haven, Connecticut, in the basement of St. Mary's Church. There the young priest assembled eighty Catholic laymen, Irish Americans like himself, who voted to launch the new group. No one, least of all Father McGivney, suspected it then, but by the second decade of the twenty-first century the Knights of Columbus would grow to be an international body of some 1.8 million Catholic men, with assets totaling over $20 billion and an influence for good to match. "Father McGivney is too modest to assume to himself any honor," one of his lay associates later said. "But if this Order succeeds

... the honor as its founder will be his." History seconds that judgment.[1]

McGivney's achievement is best appreciated in the context of nineteenth-century Irish immigration to the United States, especially the newcomers' sometimes desperate struggle to survive and flourish in the face of nativist hostility. The collision of these two powerful forces—immigration and anti-Catholic nativism—was at the center of the founding of the Knights.

By 1820 the Catholic population of the United States numbered a modest 120,000. And then the great explosion began. In the half century that followed, 2.7 million Catholic immigrants entered the country. By 1900 there were 12 million American Catholics—an astonishing hundredfold increase.

Not all the immigrants came from Ireland, but very many did. Their numbers rose rapidly—52,000 in the 1820s; 171,000 in the 1830s; 656,000 in the decade that followed; over a million in the decade after that. They struggled to put down roots, and in time they succeeded— indeed, as their German American coreligionists saw it, succeeded rather too well.

The less than edifying story of German Catholic–Irish Catholic conflict in those years is a crucial, but seldom told, chapter in the history of American Catholicism. In a sermon in 1871 James Cardinal Gibbons of Baltimore, Irish American leader of the U.S. bishops, hailed the Irish diaspora as central to God's providential plan that the Irish should play a key role in "the establishment and

[1] Biographical information about Father McGivney and specifics about the early days of the Knights of Columbus are drawn largely from Christopher J. Kauffman, *Faith and Fraternalism: The History of the Knights of Columbus, 1882–1982* (New York: Harper and Row, 1982). Unless otherwise indicated, quotations are from this source.

prosperity of the greatest Republic in the world".[2] But the success of the Irish also included growing domination of the structures of the Church. By 1880, Irish American bishops were 60 percent of the U.S. hierarchy, and in St. Louis, where German American priests outnumbered Irish American priests, all but one of the dozen men named bishops between 1854 and 1922 were Irish.

The first of the Irish to arrive were relatively well-off and mostly Protestant. But by midcentury, with Ireland in the grip of famine and dire poverty, the newcomers were overwhelmingly Catholic, poor, and sometimes unruly. They were greeted with suspicion and rejection that could easily turn violent. In 1834, an Ursuline convent outside Boston was burned to the ground by an angry mob. In the years that followed, anti-Catholic, anti-Irish violence flared in other cities.

A historian sums up the situation like this: "To Americans, they were readily perceived as drunken, boisterous threats to stability and civility and feared as henchmen of a foreign power. To American and French émigré clergy they tended to stand as constant symbols of embarrassment. Many were ... willing to take on the heaviest of workloads as wood haulers, canal diggers, railroaders, miners, and stevedores. Their situations were often so desperate that death stalked them from the 'coffin ships' to the tenement houses, where childhood mortality rates ran shockingly high."[3]

Starting from these inauspicious beginnings, the Irish would become what they are today—a well-educated,

[2]James Gibbons, "The Apostolic Mission of the Irish Race", St. Patrick's sermon preached March 17, 1871, in *A Retrospect of Fifty Years* (Baltimore: John Murphy, 1916), 2:177.

[3]Dolores R. Liptak, R.S.M., *Immigrants and Their Church* (New York: Macmillan, 1989), 76.

affluent, and influential presence in American society and the Church. In the middle decades of the nineteenth century, however, the picture was vastly different. Priests like Michael McGivney who wished to promote the interests of their Church and their people had their work cut out for them.

Michael McGivney was born August 12, 1852, in Waterbury, Connecticut, oldest of thirteen children of an immigrant couple named Patrick and Mary Lynch McGivney. His father worked as a molder in a Waterbury brass mill. Six of Michael's brothers and sisters died in infancy or childhood. A quick learner whose school principal praised his "excellent deportment and proficiency in his studies", the boy nevertheless found it necessary to leave school at age thirteen in order to help support his family by working in the spoon-making section of a brass factory. At sixteen, however, feeling an attraction to the priesthood, he left the factory and, accompanied by his pastor, traveled to Quebec to commence preparatory studies for entering the seminary there. He was attending seminary in Montreal when his father died in June 1873. Following further studies at St. Mary's Seminary in Baltimore, he was ordained in December 1877 by Archbishop (later Cardinal) Gibbons. His first assignment was at St. Mary's parish in New Haven.

St. Mary's, the first Catholic church in the city, was located in a fashionable neighborhood bordering the New Haven Green, Yale University, and a cluster of handsome Protestant houses of worship. How Catholics were then regarded was brutally apparent from the headline on a story about St. Mary's that appeared on July 27, 1879, in the *New York Times* that was subtitled "How an Aristocratic Avenue Was Blemished by a Roman Church Edifice".

The young priest busied himself with youth work until something else, something largely neglected, caught his attention: the need for a Catholic men's benevolent organization. Such an organization, with a death benefit feature providing financial support to families whose breadwinners died young, as his own father had, would be a way of keeping the men themselves out of the clutches of anti-Catholic secret societies. The idea came at a providential moment, for this was the golden age of American fraternal societies and similar groups, with some six hundred of these having already come into existence by Father McGivney's day. The first one intended specifically for the Irish, the Ancient Order of Hibernians, had been established in the United States in 1836. Others soon followed.

After exploring various options, including the creation of a local branch of some existing group, the priest and his lay associates eventually decided on a brand new organization—a "cooperative benefit order" to be called the Knights of Columbus. The name was symbolically significant. "Columbus"—Father McGivney's own suggestion—was a response to bigots who sought to deny Catholics a place in America, a verbal reminder that it was a Catholic, Christopher Columbus, who was the European discoverer of the New World. As for "Knights"—urged by men who in some cases were veterans of military service in the Civil War—the word declared the members' commitment to a kind of chivalrous crusade for the defense of their Church in the face of anti-Catholic, anti-Irish sentiment.

The first public notice of the Knights' founding appeared on February 8, 1882, in reports in the *New Haven Morning Journal* and *New Haven Courier* recording that the Knights of Columbus (K of C) had held its first meeting the night before. On March 29 the Connecticut state legislature granted the group a charter formally establishing it as a legal corporation. Its stated principles were "unity" and "charity"; later these were joined by "fraternity" and "patriotism". In April, with the permission of the bishop of Hartford, Father McGivney wrote a letter to all pastors in the diocese urging them to consider establishing K of C councils in their parishes. In May he installed the first officers of San Salvador Council 1 in New Haven.

McGivney accepted the office of secretary, though later he switched to the less time-consuming post of supreme chaplain. He traveled widely in Connecticut promoting the new group and carried on an extensive correspondence on its behalf, while also keeping up his parish duties. In these early days, says Christopher J. Kauffman in his history of the K of C, the Knights' leaders "confronted severe criticism, experienced deep disillusionment, and seriously doubted the value of their efforts". Kauffman credits the organization's survival to Father McGivney's "persistence and optimism".

Two years after the founding, Father McGivney was named pastor of St. Thomas Church in Thomaston, Connecticut, a factory town ten miles from Waterbury. Responsibility for a second parish also came with the job. Working alone, he carried a backbreaking pastoral load yet managed to continue defending and promoting the Knights.

In January 1890 he contracted pneumonia. He had never been physically robust, and in the months that followed his health declined. On August 14, only thirty-eight years old, Michael J. McGivney died. His funeral, celebrated in his hometown of Waterbury, was one of the largest in its history, with the diocesan bishop and more than seventy priests participating along with civic leaders and a large crowd, as well as delegations from most of the fifty-seven Knights of Columbus councils that had been chartered up to then. In 1982, when the Knights marked their one hundredth anniversary, his remains were transferred from

Waterbury to New Haven. Today they rest in St. Mary's Church, where the Knights of Columbus began.

The process that could one day lead to formal recognition of Father McGivney as a saint was begun in 1996. At this time he has the title "Venerable". At the group's 2013 convention K of C Supreme Knight Carl A. Anderson reported that a possible miracle worked through his intercession was being studied by the Vatican's congregation for saints.

Little short of miraculous in its own way has been the growth of the Knights of Columbus itself. Overwhelmingly Irish in the early days, today's 1.8 million Knights are an ethnically and racially diverse body, with members in the United States, Canada, Mexico, the Philippines, the Caribbean, Central America, and lately Poland, Ukraine, Lithuania, and South Korea. As of 2014, besides its $20 billion in assets, the K of C boasted over $94 billion of insurance in force on members and members' families under its highly rated insurance program, and the Knights ranked 909th in *Fortune* magazine's list of America's thousand largest companies.

This material success fuels an impressive program of charity and good works. At the national and international levels, the group gives away millions of dollars every year, including several million annually to the pope and the Holy See. But the record is even more remarkable at the grassroots, where during the 2013–2014 fraternal year members gave more than $170 million to good causes, besides contributing well over 70.5 million hours in volunteer service with an estimated value of $1.6 billion. At all levels—international, national, and local—the Knights of Columbus is a major source of financial and moral support for countless worthy projects. One historic example is the organization's funding for litigation that led in 1925 to a landmark Supreme Court ruling, *Pierce v. Society of Sisters*, overturning an Oregon law backed by anti-Catholic interests that sought to make attendance at public schools mandatory and affirming the right of parents to choose nonpublic schools for their children.

From the start, patriotism has been a major component of the K of C program. In fact, it's the special theme of the group's Fourth Degree—the men in capes and plumed hats who are a picturesque presence at many Church events. According to Kauffman, this emphasis on patriotism is a reminder that the group in its early days "provided first- and second-generation immigrants a 'rite of passage' into American society" making it "a classic instance of a minority's drive to assimilate".

Undoubtedly true. Yet in recent years a significant change has been underway in the Knights. Fidelity to Catholic beliefs and values has moved the historically Americanist and assimilationist group to adopt an increasingly countercultural stance toward a secular culture rapidly becoming more hostile to the Church and what it stands for. This is true especially on issues such as abortion, marriage, and the defense of religious liberty, where their strongly held commitment to human life and their defense of the First Amendment's guarantee of religious free exercise make the Knights an important part of the pro-life movement, while their support for traditional marriage places them in opposition to the redefinition of marriage pushed by gay rights advocates.

It seems safe to say Father McGivney would have expected no less of his Knights.

JAMES CARDINAL GIBBONS
(1834–1921)

"A Politician in the Best Sense"

H. L. Mencken, writer, journalist, and professional cur-
mudgeon, took a dim view of the clergy along with much
else. But when it came to James Cardinal Gibbons, archbishop of Baltimore for forty-four crucial years, Mencken's
iconoclasm gave way to something almost like admiration.
Writing after the cardinal's death in 1921, the Sage of Baltimore declared that "more presidents than one sought
the counsel of Cardinal Gibbons ... a man of the highest
sagacity, a politician in the best sense". There was "no
record", the Sage added, of the late prelate's having "ever
led the Church into a bog or up a blind alley".[1]

High praise, considering the source.

Mencken was hardly the cardinal's only admirer. In a
long, fruitful career, during much of which he was the
acknowledged leader of the American hierarchy, James
Gibbons combined diplomacy, patriotism, and a canny
understanding of human nature in a manner that not only
earned him recognition but made him probably the most

[1] The indispensable source of information about Gibbons and the Catholic
Church in America in his day is John Tracy Ellis' monumental two-volume
biography, *The Life of James Cardinal Gibbons* (Milwaukee: Bruce Publishing,
1952). Perhaps fittingly, Monsignor Ellis shares Gibbons' Americanist views.
Unless otherwise indicated, quotations are from this source.

effective advocate, before or since, of the Americanization of American Catholicism. Gibbons believed with all his heart that the nation he loved provided a congenial home for the Church that he loved. In a sermon in Rome in 1887, he unabashedly affirmed his "deep sense of pride and gratitude" for the blessing of American freedom that had allowed Catholicism to thrive. To him, perhaps more than anyone else, the Catholic Church in America owes both the advantages and the unanticipated drawbacks of assimilation into American culture.

James Gibbons was born in Baltimore on July 23, 1834, the fourth of six children of Thomas and Bridget Gibbons, an Irish immigrant couple from County Mayo. In 1839, suffering from tuberculosis and hoping the move would benefit his health, his father, a grocer, took the family back to Ireland. After the elder Gibbons' death, mother and children returned to the United States and settled in New Orleans.

Feeling drawn to the priesthood, young James entered the seminary in Baltimore in 1855 and was ordained in 1861. After pastoral assignments that included Civil War service as volunteer chaplain of Baltimore's historic Fort McHenry, the birthplace of the Star-Spangled Banner, he was appointed secretary to Archbishop Martin John Spalding. In that capacity the young man assisted in the preparations for the Second Plenary Council of Baltimore.

In 1868, responding to a request from that plenary assembly of the U.S. bishops, Pope Pius IX established a new quasi-diocesan jurisdiction in North Carolina called an apostolic vicariate, appointed Gibbons to head it, and named him a bishop. In 1872 he was transferred to Richmond as its fourth ordinary while remaining in charge of the North Carolina vicariate. Catholics were few and far between in North Carolina and Virginia in those years, and, traveling widely in both states to visit his scattered flock, the young bishop encountered many Protestants, sometimes even preaching in their churches. The experience provided him with material for a work of apologetics, *Faith of Our Fathers*, published in 1876. The book became one of the leading religious best sellers of all time and even today is still reprinted and read.

The volume was something more than apologetics, however. In a manner reminiscent of Isaac Hecker, the young bishop aspired to attract Protestants to the Catholic Church. Noting that Scripture speaks of Christ's Church "by the beautiful title of bride or spouse of Christ", Gibbons underlined his point: "and the Christian law admits only of one wife". He went on: "With all due respect for my dissenting brethren, truth compels me to say that this unity of doctrine and government is not to be found in the Protestant sects, taken collectively or separately.... Where, then shall we find this essential unity of faith and government? I answer, confidently, nowhere save in the Catholic Church."[2] This was surprisingly aggressive for so mild-mannered a man as the author.

At the First Vatican Council, which took place in 1869–1870, Bishop Gibbons was the second youngest bishop—and youngest from the United States; he voted there in favor of defining the dogma of papal infallibility. In May 1877 Pope Pius named him coadjutor archbishop of Baltimore. Following the death of the incumbent a few months later, he became archbishop.

Students of Gibbons' life and career find many qualities to praise. Monsignor Ellis, his biographer, lists among these the habit of consulting before making decisions,

---

[2]James Cardinal Gibbons, *The Faith of Our Fathers* (Amsterdam: Fredonia Books, 2004), 6–7.

consideration for others' feelings, a "naturally irenic temperament", balanced judgment, and keen intelligence. But he also had faults, including a certain vanity regarding the perks and prerogatives of his office and—a frequent source of frustration to impetuous colleagues like the flamboyant Archbishop John Ireland of St. Paul—a marked tendency to hesitance and indecisiveness in making up his mind and taking a stand.[3]

Although the office of archbishop of Baltimore, the oldest diocese in the United States, made him de facto primate of the American hierarchy, only in presiding successfully at the Third Plenary Council of Baltimore in 1884 did Gibbons emerge as a genuinely national figure. At first unconvinced that such a meeting of bishops was really needed, he eventually became a strong supporter of the third council in Baltimore and its program for the rapidly expanding Catholic Church in the United States. In 1886, Pope Leo named him a cardinal, only the second American to be so honored.

At the time, the Holy See, beleaguered by anticlerical governments in Italy, France, and Germany, held a more than mildly skeptical view of the separation of church and state existing in the United States. Thus it was an act of uncharacteristic bravado for Gibbons, preaching in Santa Maria Trastevere, his titular church in Rome, to deliver a (for him) bold and provocative defense of American church-state arrangements.[4] Noting that Pope Leo XIII had lately published an encyclical, *Immortale Dei*, in which the pope remarked that the Church had succeeded in adapting

---

[3] For Tracy Ellis' summing-up on Gibbons, see *Life* 2:633ff.

[4] "The Roman Sermon of the American Cardinal on Church and State in the United States, March 25, 1887", in *Documents of American Catholic History*, ed. John Tracy Ellis (Milwaukee: Bruce Publishing, 1962), 457–59.

itself to many forms of government over the centuries, the new American cardinal said: "She has lived under absolute empires; she thrives under constitutional monarchies; she grows and expands under the free republic.... In the genial air of liberty, she blossoms like the rose!"

"For myself," Gibbons continued, "as a citizen of the United States, without closing my eyes to our defects as a nation, I proclaim, with a deep sense of pride and gratitude, and in this great capitol of Christendom, that I belong to a country where the civil government holds over us the aegis of its protection without interfering in the legitimate exercise of our sublime mission as ministers of the Gospel of Jesus Christ."

So much for Roman skepticism about church-state separation in the American manner. Isaac Hecker would have been proud.

As primate of the American hierarchy and wearer of the red hat, Cardinal Gibbons in the years that followed was repeatedly called on to take a central part in the vexing issues that confronted American Catholicism. His finest hour may have been his timely backing for the organized labor movement in its infancy.

Leading the way at the start was a group called the Knights of Labor. It had many Catholic working men as members and was headed by a Catholic, Terence V. Powderly. At the Vatican, however, the Knights of Labor were viewed with suspicion as a secret society. And since secret societies were then causing much grief to the Church in Europe, a papal condemnation forbidding Catholics to belong to the new American group seemed likely.

At that point Gibbons weighed in with a lengthy memorial to Rome defending the Knights and arguing that the Church should stand with the workers. Unlike the situation in many places in Europe, he wrote, the Church in

America enjoyed widespread popular support; it would be self-destructive folly to jeopardize that by an ill-timed and unnecessary condemnation of a workingmen's organization with significant Catholic membership. Said Gibbons: "There is the evident danger of the Church's losing in popular estimation her right to be considered a friend of the people.... To lose the heart of the people would be a misfortune for which the friendship of the few rich and powerful would be no compensation."[5]

Not only was there no papal condemnation, but historians consider Gibbons' intervention to have been of critical importance in maintaining friendly relations between the Church and the American labor movement, besides helping to shape Pope Leo's historic social encyclical of 1891, *Rerum Novarum*.

Keeping the Catholic University of America afloat was another challenge that tested the cardinal's mettle. Among the decisions of the Third Plenary Council had been the creation of a national university under the bishops' sponsorship. Following protracted episcopal wrangling, Washington, D.C., was finally chosen as the site. Typically cool to the project at the start, Gibbons eventually became a zealous supporter. In 1904, after the university's investments turned sour and the very survival of the school was threatened, his lobbying of his fellow bishops for financial help was crucial to saving the young school.

Energetic patriotism was an important part of Gibbons' program for the Americanization of Catholics. As tensions over Cuba mounted in the 1890s between the United States and Catholic Spain, the cardinal sought to head off a military clash, but when peace efforts failed and the Spanish-American War broke out, he lined up foursquare

---

[5] "Cardinal Gibbons' Defense of the Knights of Labor", in ibid., 449.

on the side of America. Twenty years later, unconditional patriotism again colored his reaction to World War I. In April 1917, on the eve of a congressional declaration of war on Germany, Gibbons published a statement containing the remarkable assertion that "absolute and unreserved obedience to his country's call" was a citizen's first duty. While this mirrored sentiments widely shared by war-minded Americans at the time, it would be virtually impossible today to find responsible theologians or Christian religious leaders whose view of the duties of citizenship extends that far.

Inevitably, during the closing years of the century, Cardinal Gibbons was embroiled in another tangled controversy with the Holy See focused on the phenomenon known to history as "Americanism". Central to it was an assortment of ideas then current among liberal Catholics in France and some other European countries, which the Vatican not only deplored but considered to be linked to U.S. Catholicism. Gibbons and his friends—men like Ireland of St. Paul; John Keane, rector of the Catholic University of America; and the cardinal's agent in Rome, Denis O'Connell—scrambled to head off a papal condemnation. But this time they failed. In January 1899 Pope Leo XIII published a document, written in the form of a letter to Gibbons and titled *Testem Benevolentiae* ("Witness to Good Will"), that came down hard on Americanism, saying it "raises a suspicion that there are those among you who envision and desire a Church in America other than that which is in all the rest of the world".[6]

---

[6] Pope Leo XIII, Letter *Testem Benevolentiae* to the Archbishop of Baltimore, in *Compendium of Creeds, Definitions, and Declarations on Matters of Faith and Morals*, ed. Heinrich Denziger, Peter Hünermann, Robert Fastiggi, and Anne Englund Nash (San Francisco: Ignatius Press, 2012), 3346.

Although historians sympathetic to the Americanists dismiss the significance of the papal document, someone reading it now with unbiased eyes will find it a remarkably prescient warning against trends and attitudes that have done more than their share to sap the strength of American Catholicism. These include support for a version of religious life largely cut off from supernatural roots and the idea that everyone is entitled to his own opinion in matters religious, thanks to direct inspiration by the Holy Spirit as if by "a kind of hidden instinct".

Appalled at the papal condemnation, the archbishop of Baltimore replied for the record with a formal letter to Leo XIII thanking him profusely for his message while assuring him that no one in America held the views the pope had just condemned. Gibbons wrote: "This doctrine, which I deliberately call extravagant and absurd, this Americanism as it has been called, has nothing in common with the views, aspirations, doctrine and conduct of Americans. I do not think that there can be found in the entire country a bishop, a priest, or even a layman with a knowledge of his religion who has ever uttered such enormities."

Ever the careful diplomat, however, Gibbons made it a point to express appreciation for Leo's distinction between the "enormities"—which American Catholics unhesitatingly joined the pope in condemning—and "those feelings of love for our country and its institutions which we share with our fellow citizens and which are such a powerful aid in accomplishing our work."

In fairness to the cardinal, it should be said that he was not an Americanist in the sense Pope Leo meant. But that no one else was is not so clear. Today, in any case, very many are.

But that was to be in the future. In his own day, when millions of Catholic immigrants and their children were making the great transition from immigrant status to incorporation into American culture—to their benefit and the benefit of their Church, as it seemed—the achievement of James Gibbons in helping make that happen was widely recognized and rightly applauded. Not long before his death, his good friend Theodore Roosevelt called him "the most useful citizen of our country". From the American point of view, Teddy Roosevelt may have been right.

SAINT FRANCES XAVIER
CABRINI (1850–1917)

"I Worked on Mr. Capitano Pizzati
for a Month"

Prior to the great surge of Hispanic immigration in the last several decades, historians commonly spoke of four main periods of Catholic immigration to America identified with four ethnic groups: the Irish (new arrivals from Ireland peaked in the 1850s), the Germans (in the 1880s), the Italians (early 1900s), and the Poles and other Slavs (1920s). The immigrant experience, including entry into the Catholic Church as the newcomers found it here, was in some ways different for each of them but more or less trying for all.

And for none more trying than it was for the Italians.

Between 1880 and 1920, as many as four million of them came to America, most from poverty-ridden southern Italy. Many were temporary workers—"builders of bridges, tunnels, and subways, longshoremen and factory workers", one writer says—who came to earn money and, that done, often hurried back to Italy.[1] (By 1910 the

---

[1] Information about Mother Cabrini and Italian immigration is drawn largely from Dolores Liptak, R.S.M., *Immigrants and Their Church* (New York: Macmillan, 1989), 142–59. Unless otherwise noted, Mother Cabrini quotations are from this source.

number of those who did that was estimated to be as high as eight hundred thousand.) But many more stayed and made new homes here. Or at least, in the face of serious obstacles, they tried.

Early in those years, Frances Cabrini had met with Pope Leo XIII and told him of her dream to go to China as a missionary. "No," the pope answered, "not to the East but to the West." He wanted Cabrini and her recently founded Missionary Sisters of the Sacred Heart to go to America and do pastoral work among the Italian immigrants there.

Mother Cabrini and her sisters went. What happened after that is a bright page in the sometimes tumultuous story of Italian American Catholicism. In 1946, the heroic love of God and neighbor that motivated her was formally recognized by the Church—she was declared a saint. That made her the first U.S. citizen to be canonized—although, a historian says, she remained "Italian ... to the very marrow of her bones."

Francesca Cabrini was born July 15, 1850, in Sant'Angelo Lodigiano, a town in Lombardy, the youngest of thirteen children in a well-off farming family. A pious child—the "little saint", neighbors called her—she longed to be a missionary and played at sailing paper boats filled with violets representing the sisters she meant to send all over the world. But her father had other ideas, and after studying to be a teacher she taught school.

On two occasions, she sought admission to religious orders but was refused—supposedly for poor health but in reality, it seems, because a local monsignor had something else in mind for her: he wanted her to take over direction of a troubled orphanage. Francesca did, and after she had run the orphanage for six years, the local bishop asked her and her companions to organize themselves as a religious community. The Missionary Sisters had been born, with the foundress taking Frances Xavier as her religious name—"Xavier" for the sixteenth-century Jesuit missionary to the Far East, Saint Francis Xavier.

Although the new order was only a diocesan institute at first, Mother Cabrini had larger plans from the start. After establishing new convents in Cremona and Milan, she went to Rome to seek papal approval and also, she hoped, open a convent there. At first the cardinal in charge of such matters said no—Rome had enough convents already—but this determined woman of great charm persisted, and in the end the cardinal allowed her to open not just one convent but two.

It was around this time that she had the life-changing interview with Leo XIII that sent her on her way to the United States. Already in 1884 the American bishops at the Third Plenary Council of Baltimore had discussed the desperate pastoral situation of the Italian immigrants. Little came of that discussion at first, but now at least the "Italian problem" was formally recognized as a problem for the Church at large.

And a serious problem it was. New York, for instance, had some fifty thousand Italians, but according to New York's Archbishop Michael Corrigan, hardly more than 2 percent of them ever went to church. The newcomers' problems included poverty, a critical shortage of Italian-speaking priests, habits of anticlericalism, and spotty religious practice that they brought with them from the old country, as well as pervasive anti-Italian feeling existing not only among non-Catholics but also among American Catholics.

At the heart of their troubles was a clash of cultures between the Italians and the Irish Americans who dominated the ecclesiastical infrastructure. That some of these immigrants nevertheless managed to practice the faith,

Sister Dolores Liptak, a historian of the immigrant experience, remarks drily, was surely not due to "their being understood or well-treated either by American Catholics or Americans generally".

Deeply disturbed at the "toilsome and disastrous condition" of his fellow Italians, Pope Leo in December 1888 sent the U.S. bishops a long and passionate letter appealing for their help. Among other things, the document was remarkable for the vivid picture it painted of the position in which the Italians found themselves: "At the outset the emigrants' crossing itself is full of dangers and injuries; for many of them fall into the hands of avaricious men whose slaves, as it were, they become, and then herded in ships and inhumanly treated, they are gradually depraved in their nature. And when they have reached the desired land, being ignorant of both the language and the locale, and engrossed in their daily toil, they become the victims of the trickery of the dishonest or the powerful by whom they are employed."[2]

Even those Italians who managed to support themselves faced serious difficulties, the pope maintained. "Associating constantly with people who regard everything from the point of view of business or profit, [they] little by little lose the nobler feelings of human nature" and become like the money-grubbers around them. And of course there was the ever-present threat of Protestant proselytism—"the deceits practiced by the sects which flourish widely there ... which draw many into the path leading to destruction".

Still "more lamentable", Leo XIII told the bishops, was the lack of pastoral resources in the Catholic community,

[2] "Pope Leo XIII's Plea for the Italian Immigrants in America", in *Documents of American Catholic History*, ed. John Tracy Ellis (Milwaukee: Bruce Publishing, 1962), 463.

with a shortage of Italian-speaking priests at the top of the list. "In many places, therefore, there are very few who have a priest when they are dying, and there are many of the newly-born for whom there is none to administer [baptism]. There are many who enter into marriage without regard to the Church's laws, and thereby give rise to an offspring similar to their parents. Thus there is everywhere with this people a decay of Christian morality and a growth of wickedness."

Pope Leo's words combined with the bishops' own growing sense of the problem to produce results. A pastoral strategy began to emerge, bolstered by the arrival of new Italian religious communities like the Scalabrinian Fathers and the Pallottines as well as by training American priests to work with the Italians. The first parish in the United States specifically for them had been founded in Philadelphia in 1852, and now these spiritual enclaves where the language and devotional traditions of Italy were retained multiplied. In time, Italian parishes became a notable part of the growing body of ethnic parishes that well into the twentieth century played an important and largely beneficial role in mediating the integration of Catholic newcomers into the larger ecclesiastical and secular communities of America.

Mother Cabrini and her sisters rapidly became part of this increasingly effective program. She arrived in New York on March 31, 1889, and, after a brief period of tension with Archbishop Corrigan over where to set up shop, she and her companions settled in and got to work. Within a month, they were running an orphanage. In less than three years they had a hospital. (Mother Cabrini called all her hospitals—two in New York, two in Chicago—"Columbus Hospital". Today, all have long since closed.)

There is not enough room here to list all the orphanages, schools, hospitals, and clinics that these women—like the many thousands of women in other religious institutes who did so much to build the vast infrastructure of American Catholicism—were responsible for establishing and operating. But the numbers do at least suggest the magnitude of what Frances Cabrini and her companions accomplished. By the time she died thirty-four years after her arrival in America, the twenty-three hundred Missionary Sisters of the Sacred Heart who by then were serving in the United States and throughout the Western Hemisphere had established sixty-seven institutions devoted to the physical, moral, and spiritual welfare of people in need.

In the spirit of the little girl who dreamed years before of sending missionaries all over the world, Mother Cabrini carried on a ministry with expansive horizons. Her order spread across the United States—to Chicago, to the mining camps of Colorado, and to Sing Sing prison in New York, as well as to Mississippi, New Jersey, Pennsylvania, and Washington state. Learning that a mob in New Orleans had lately lynched some Italians accused of committing crimes, she responded by summoning several sisters from New York to begin work among the Italians of the Crescent City. But her work also extended beyond the United States. As early as September 1891 she took fourteen sisters to Nicaragua to start an academy. Argentina, Chile, France, Spain, England—Missionary Sisters went to all these places. Although Italians were not the only ones they served, Italians remained the special focus of their efforts.

Cabrini's drive and determination were astonishing. And like some other holy people deeply involved in humanitarian work—Mother Teresa comes to mind— Mother Cabrini had a hardheaded grasp of the practicalities of doing good.

Her first and most important resource was the gritty commitment of her sisters. "Work hard, my daughters, never tire, work with generosity, work with determination and generosity," she told them. But she understood very well that money was needed and wasn't shy about getting it. "I worked on Mr. Capitano Pizzati for a month," she wrote from New Orleans in 1904, "and in the end he decided to give me $50,000 over ten years. However, he wanted to see the house built right away. I told him that I could not advance the funds and that it would be better if he saw to constructing the house for us. Then he said happily, 'Well, you prepare the ground for me and I will build the house.' And he has already commissioned a $75,000 plan from the architect and it will be built immediately." Ingenuity also played a role. In Los Angeles she bought an abandoned amusement park at a bargain price and used materials from its demolition to add a new wing to her order's house.

In 1909 Mother Cabrini became a naturalized citizen of the United States. The following year, aware that her strength was failing, she announced that she intended to resign as superior general of the order and devote herself exclusively to prayer. But the houses of the Missionary Sisters voted unanimously to have her stay on. Observing those results, the cardinal-prefect of the Vatican's congregation for religious told her jokingly, "Mother Cabrini, though up to now you have governed your institute badly, I have decided to give you another chance. You are to remain superior general." Unfazed, the foundress replied, "Well, I warn you that I shall be just as severe as in the past."

She died December 22, 1917, at Columbus Hospital in Chicago. After an unusually brief interval of only twenty-one years, Pope Pius XI in 1938 declared her "blessed". Pius XII canonized her in 1946 and in 1950 designated her "Patroness of the Immigrants".

At a certain point in Edwin O'Connor's novel of big-city politics, *The Last Hurrah*, Frank Skeffingon, a mayor with a masterful grasp of ethnic realities, faces a problem. A statue is to be placed in an Italian neighborhood, and the locals are fighting over whose statue it should be. Skeffington's solution: Mother Cabrini. He explains: "Italian born, and the first American saint. Let's see them get out of that. The first man, woman, child or monsignor who objects will be stoned out of town. That's what I mean by a compromise."[3]

For a politician like Skeffington, honoring Mother Cabrini might have been a smart solution to a sticky problem, but for others it is well-deserved recognition of a brave woman who served her people, her adopted country, and her God, and served them all remarkably well.

---

[3] Edwin O'Connor, *The Last Hurrah* (New York: Bantam Books, 1956), 237.

AL SMITH
(1873–1944)

"I Am a Product of America and of American Institutions"

To Franklin Roosevelt, Al Smith was "the Happy Warrior of the political battlefield".[1] To suspicious Protestants, he was a pawn of the pope. And amid such conflicting views as these, the remarkable political career of Al Smith was forged. A four-term governor of New York and Democratic candidate for president in 1928, Smith was a living embodiment of the enormous shifts in America's cultural and political center of gravity that were taking place during his lifetime—from rural to urban, Anglo-Saxon stock to immigrant ethnic, Protestant to a pluralistic stew of Americanized religious bodies bubbling together in the melting pot of cultural assimilation.

Of particular significance to Catholics, Smith demonstrated that one of them could rise to the top of America's political heap—or at least very close to it—yet in the end still have his religion count against him. Before the presidential election of 1928, candidate Smith appealed to the

[1] Information about Smith and his political career is drawn from, among other places, John T. McGreevey, *Catholicism and American Freedom* (New York: W. W. Norton, 2003), 147–51; Theodore Maynard, *Great Catholics in American History* (New York: All Saints Press, 1962), 191–99; and William B. Prendergast, *The Catholic Voter in American Politics* (Washington, D.C.: Georgetown University Press, 1999), 93–115.

Constitution's ban on a religious test for public office in the face of an anti-Catholic barrage aimed at him and his Church. It was a "sad thing", he indignantly declared, that some self-proclaimed Americans should be calling for his defeat "because of my religious belief". For the moment, though, the bigots prevailed, thereby writing a fresh chapter in the old story of American anti-Catholicism.

Alfred Emmanuel Smith was born December 30, 1873, on the Lower East Side of Manhattan. He was to live there most of his life. At the time of his birth, the Brooklyn Bridge was under construction nearby, and Smith said later that he and the bridge "grew up together". His parents were Alfred Ferraro, son of Italian and German immigrants and himself a Civil War veteran who took the name Alfred E. Smith, and Catherine Mulvihill Smith, whose parents had come to America from Ireland's County Westmeath.

Smith's father died when the boy was thirteen, and young Al dropped out of parochial school to help support the family. He never attended high school or college, saying he had studied human nature while working at the Fulton Fish Market for twelve dollars a week. In 1900 he married Catherine Dunn. They had five children and were a notably happy couple until her death in 1944.

Having honed his speaking skills in parish theatricals, Smith took to politics. His early career was linked to Tammany Hall, New York's Democratic political machine that often was depicted as an archetype of big-city corruption. But Smith remained scandal-free throughout his career while laboring on behalf of reform causes such as government efficiency and measures to help working people and immigrants. If in 1928 even a single scandal could have been tied to him, he remarked, that would have been sufficient to ruin his chances of election; but his opponents couldn't find any scandal "because the truth is it is not there".

From 1904 to 1915 he served in the state assembly. At various times, depending on the Democrats' political fortunes, he held the offices of Majority Leader and Minority Leader as well as Speaker. In November 1915 he was elected sheriff of New York County, a position abundant in political patronage. In 1917 he became president of the city's board of aldermen.

Smith was elected governor in 1918, defeated for reelection in 1920, then reelected in 1922, 1924, and 1926. He was identified with the "progressive" movement in politics, and his years as governor saw laws enacted that dealt with issues like workmen's compensation, women's pensions, and child labor. Among his close political associates were people destined later to rise to national prominence, including James A. Farley, who managed several Smith election campaigns, planner and builder Robert Moses, and Frances Perkins, a future U.S. secretary of labor.

In 1920 and again in 1924, Smith sought the Democratic presidential nomination, and it was in the latter year that Roosevelt, in a nominating speech at the party convention, called him "the Happy Warrior of the political battlefield"—a tag that stuck. Smith and another contender then proceeded to fight it out through one hundred inconclusive ballots until the weary delegates turned to a third candidate, who was overwhelmed in November by Republican Calvin Coolidge.

Nothing daunted, Smith now set his sights on the 1928 nomination. From the start it was clear that, if and when he ran for president, he would be dogged by the religious issue.

In fact, the assault began long before he secured the nomination. In April 1927 the *Atlantic Monthly* published "An Open Letter to the Honorable Alfred E. Smith", written by a New York lawyer named Charles Marshall.

Marshall asked whether Smith shared the negative views on religious freedom expressed in some papal documents of the previous century (while endorsing tolerance of non-Catholic religions in overwhelmingly Catholic countries, popes of that era typically opposed removing the Catholic Church's special position as the officially established religion in such places). And how, Marshall demanded, would Smith approach the apparently opposed claims of the secular state and the Catholic Church with respect to the education of children?

Smith's reply was written with the assistance of Father Francis Patrick Duffy, a close friend who had served as chaplain of New York's famous "Fighting 69th" regiment in World War I. The *Atlantic Monthly* rushed it into print, and it appeared the following month. In effect, Smith shrugged off Marshall's dark speculations about Catholics in public office, noting that in his long experience as a public official there had been no conflict between his faith and his official duties, and the record of American Catholics' loyal service to the nation deserved to be given more weight than abstract quarrels about "dogmatic principles".

Although some Catholics were miffed at Smith for his casual approach to Church teaching ("I never heard of these bulls and encyclicals and books"), it was commonly agreed that he had successfully vindicated his right to contest for the presidency. The liberal *New Republic* judged that the episode left reasonable Americans no basis for "refusing to support him on the pretext of his Catholicism".

Unfortunately, it appeared that not all Americans were reasonable. The Ku Klux Klan, refounded in 1915, was riding high in those days, with Blacks, Jews, and Catholics as the special targets of its vitriol. A U.S. senator, Thomas Heflin of Alabama, made a name for himself by denouncing "the Roman hierarchy and the political machine" while promoting talks by former nuns who had supposedly "escaped" from their convents. Oregon adopted a law sought by Masons whose intended effect would have been the closing of parochial schools.[2] In such ways as these the stage was set for an ugly campaign if Smith sought the nation's highest office.

On June 28, 1928, at the Democratic convention in Houston, Smith received the party's nomination for president on the first ballot. While the race that followed demonstrated that America had traveled a long way from the religious bigotry of the nineteenth century, it also demonstrated that the country still had far to go to make the Constitution's ban on a religious test for public office a universal reality. An editorial in a Protestant magazine declaring "the mere mention of a Roman Catholic as President" to be a cause for alarm was typical of the tone and substance of the religiously grounded opposition Smith now encountered. The writer warned that, with Smith in the presidential race, "Rome has reached one of its long-sought goals." And now: "It well behooves us to emphasize before our people those cardinal principles which came forth as fruit of the Reformation, on which our government is founded.... Rome has not changed.... Eternal vigilance is the price of liberty."

On September 20, speaking in Oklahoma City, Smith delivered a passionate response to his critics. So fierce was the local hostility to the candidate and so blunt were his remarks that contemporary accounts reported real concern for his safety.

But Smith was undeterred. After a lengthy look back at his unblemished record as a public servant, the candidate

[2] The Supreme Court unanimously overturned this law in 1925. See the chapter above on Father Michael McGivney and the Knights of Columbus.

came to the matter at hand—his religion and the opposition to his candidacy it had evoked. Saying he'd been told that "politically it might be expedient for me to remain silent on this subject", he flatly rejected the idea of doing that. "No political expediency will keep me from speaking out in an endeavor to destroy these evil attacks" directed against him because of his faith, he proclaimed.

"I can think of no greater disaster to this country," Smith declared, "than to have the voters ... divide upon religious lines. It is contrary to the spirit, not only of the Declaration of Independence, but of the Constitution itself.... Our forefathers, in their wisdom, wrote into the Constitution of the United States that no religious test shall ever be applied for public office." And this was "not a mere form of words" but "the most vital principle that ever was given to any people".

"I attack those who seek to undermine it," Smith concluded, "not only because I am a good Christian, but because I am a good American and a product of America and of American institutions. Everything I am, and everything I hope to be, I owe to those institutions."

Even today it is impossible to read Smith's words without being moved. But in the end his fierce eloquence hardly mattered to the outcome. A month and a half later, he lost to Herbert Hoover in a landslide, collecting 40.77 percent of the popular vote and 87 electoral votes to the Republican's 58.2 percent and 444 electoral votes.

It is likely that no Democrat, Catholic or not, could have won that year—the Republicans were too identified with the prosperity of the 1920s for that to happen. Moreover, other issues besides religion played roles in Smith's defeat, including his opposition to Prohibition and his image as a fast-talking New Yorker. (The use of "East Side, West Side" as his campaign song didn't help.) Smith's

Catholicism even paid some dividends by bringing him the Catholic vote (80 percent), including the votes of many Catholic women who'd never voted before. Overall, however, religion worked against him, with traditionally Democratic states such as Texas, Oklahoma, and Florida all going Republican. The *New York Times* concluded that countless votes were cast against Smith "because he was a Catholic". That remains the consensus today.

His defeat made a powerful impact on the psyches of American Catholics, whose red-hot anger mingled with a frustrated yearning for acceptance by non-Catholics. More than two decades later, those feelings were central motifs in a best-selling novel called *The Cardinal*. The book, by Catholic writer Henry Morton Robinson, is a highly romanticized but thinly disguised version of the career of Francis Cardinal Spellman of New York. Speaking of the events of 1928, Robinson attributes to his hero, a rising young churchman named Stephen Fermoyle, these bitter reflections: "Would [critics of the Church] never realize that Catholicism in the United States was a cornerstone of civil order, a bulwark against the corrupting forces of anarchy and decay? To those who accused the Church of undermining American freedom, Stephen wanted to cry out: 'Our sole aim is to inculcate patriotism founded upon divine law ... to help men keep alive the light of their souls, the hope of heaven, the love of God.'"[3]

Smith was eager for another shot at the White House in the election of 1932, but the Democrats turned instead to Roosevelt. Smith supported him during the campaign but later became a critic of FDR's New Deal policies, and relations between the two men soured. Practically

[3] Henry Morton Robinson, *The Cardinal* (New York: Simon and Schuster, 1950), 74. See the following chapter about Francis Cardinal Spellman.

speaking, this was the end of Smith's political career. Meanwhile, though, he had become president of Empire State, Inc., the corporation responsible for constructing the Empire State Building, and presided over the management of what was then the world's tallest building. His close ties with this iconic structure supplied an appropriate winding-down for the career of a man who'd always been a New Yorker at heart.

Al Smith died on October 4, 1944, just five months after his beloved wife, Catherine. Bitter recollections of the campaign of 1928 lingered in the memories of American Catholics for decades after that. One long-term result of Smith's defeat and of the bigotry that helped bring it about was the mobilization of Catholics as a formidable force in national politics. As events were to show, the great beneficiary of that would be another Catholic politician: John F. Kennedy.

FRANCIS CARDINAL SPELLMAN
(1889–1967)

"American and Roman"

Many cardinals have had books written about them, but not many have been the fictionalized heroes of best-selling novels. Francis Cardinal Spellman, archbishop of New York from 1939 to 1967, was one—possibly the only one.

The Cardinal, the work of Catholic author Henry Morton Robinson, topped the best-seller list for many months after its publication in 1950. Later it was made into a movie—which, however, jazzed up the story line with the box office in view. But despite their many embellishments, both book and movie in part at least mirrored the real-life career of Cardinal Spellman—hard-fought climb to the top of the hierarchical ladder, trusted advisor to a pope and a president, behind-the-scenes unofficial diplomat engaged in sensitive wartime missions. Henry Morton Robinson's purple prose summed it all up like this: "Possessor of a mind seasoned by reality and fortified by long experience of men and affairs, Stephen Fermoyle [the novel's Spellman look-alike] was the ripe product of religious faith, spiritual discipline, and intellectual energy."[1]

When *Time* magazine, marking Francis Spellman's elevation to cardinal, featured his cherubic features on the

---

[1] Henry Morton Robinson, *The Cardinal* (New York: Simon and Schuster, 1950), 509.

cover of its February 25, 1946, issue, the artist placed the dome of St. Peter's Basilica and a spire of St. Patrick's Cathedral in the background. He might also have included the White House. For Cardinal Spellman, operating at the uppermost levels of church and state, embodied the fusion of Americanism and Catholicism that had been taking shape for a century and just then was reaching its culmination.

Robinson's page-turning novel is a product of popular art whose interest today lies not so much in what it tells us about Cardinal Spellman (which is probably not very much) as in its idealized portrait of an American prince of the Church. Considered in this light, the book provides a larger-than-life picture of the achievements, aspirations, and anxieties of Catholics in mid-twentieth century America. In many respects this was the high point of American Catholicism up until now, and in presenting a heightened version of the Spellman story *The Cardinal* makes abundantly clear both the strengths and the weaknesses of American Catholicism in that short-lived era of its soaring pride and vaunting aspiration.

Francis Joseph Spellman was born May 4, 1889, in Whitman, Massachusetts, the oldest of five children of William and Ellen Conway Spellman.[2] His father was a grocer, and both parents were of Irish ancestry. Young Francis attended the local high school, where he was manager of the baseball team. From there he went on to Fordham University in New York, graduating in 1911. By then he'd decided to become a priest.

As a seminarian of the Boston archdiocese, he studied at the Urban College in Rome, exhibiting a talent for

---

[2]Biographical information about Cardinal Spellman is drawn largely from Gerald P. Fogarty, S.J., "Francis Spellman: American and Roman", in *Patterns of Episcopal Leadership* (New York: Macmillan, 1989), 216–34. Unless otherwise noted, quotations are from this source.

cultivating friendships with men who in time were to rise to high positions in the Roman Curia. Ordained a priest in 1916, he returned to Boston. There he appears to have had some kind of falling-out with William Cardinal O'Connell, the imperious and autocratic churchman who ruled the archdiocese with an iron hand. Whatever may have been the cause of the rupture, young Father Spellman was obliged to spend the next several years in a series of insignificant temporary assignments.

Even so, he kept up his Roman contacts. The breakthrough came for him in 1925, when he accompanied a pilgrimage group to Rome. While there, he took the opportunity to secure a post in the Vatican Secretariat of State and obtain the position of director of several Roman playgrounds that had been funded by America's Knights of Columbus at the request of Pope Pius XI as a bulwark against Fascist inroads among Catholic youth. He also made friends—with wealthy American Catholics; with Count Enrico Galeazzi, a layman and consummate Vatican insider; and with Archbishop (soon to be Cardinal) Eugenio Pacelli, the Holy See's nuncio to Germany, whom Pius XI named his secretary of state in 1929.

Father Spellman's opportunity to shine came in 1931. The pope had issued an encyclical sharply critical of Benito Mussolini's Fascist regime, but the Fascists refused to allow its publication in Italy. His superiors assigned the young American priest to smuggle the document to Paris, where it received international media attention. His reward came the following year when he was named auxiliary bishop of Boston and ordained in St. Peter's by Cardinal Pacelli. With the approval of Pope Pius, he adopted the pope's episcopal motto as his own: *Sequere Deum*—"Follow God".

Bishop Spellman may have been a hero in Rome, but it was a different story back home in Boston. Cardinal

O'Connell hadn't asked for an auxiliary bishop—and certainly not this one. The cardinal therefore sent his unsought auxiliary into an ecclesiastical equivalent of exile—a parish assignment that brought him as little public visibility as possible. But Bishop Spellman was not so easily thwarted. With funding from his friend Joseph P. Kennedy, a Boston multimillionaire and father of a future president, he organized the 1936 U.S. visit of his close Roman friend, Cardinal Pacelli, and accompanied the Vatican secretary of state on his cross-country tour, flying in an airliner chartered by Kennedy. A high point of the trip was a meeting, arranged by Bishop Spellman, between the cardinal and President Franklin Roosevelt at Roosevelt's Hyde Park, New York, estate.

On September 4, 1938, Patrick Cardinal Hayes of New York passed away. Pope Pius XI died the following February 10, and on March 2 the cardinals gathered in conclave and elected Cardinal Pacelli to succeed him. He took the name Pius XII. On April 24 the Holy See announced that the auxiliary bishop of Boston had been appointed archbishop of New York. The first person besides family members whom archbishop-elect Spellman notified was President Roosevelt.

As the world plunged into war and the United States edged toward entering the conflict, Roosevelt more and more turned to Archbishop Spellman as an advisor on Catholic affairs. At the end of 1939, Pope Pius named him to the post of military vicar—prelate of an ecclesiastical entity resembling a diocese that was responsible for the pastoral care of Catholics in the armed forces. (Today it is called the military archdiocese.) Not only did this role heighten his national and international profile, as the nation moved toward war, a historian writes, he more and more "closely identified Catholicism and American patriotism".

There was of course ample precedent for doing this in the policy and practice of the American hierarchy of the past. Although Cardinal Gibbons and his colleagues, acting at the urging of the Vatican, had tried a half century earlier to head off a U.S. war with Catholic Spain, once the Spanish-American War broke out, there was no doubting the bishops' foursquare support for the United States in the hostilities. Gibbons similarly endorsed American entry into World War I and actively backed President Wilson's war policy. Now it was Archbishop Spellman's turn.

Henry Morton Robinson translates all this into fictional terms in a remarkable passage that concludes his novel. Fully to understand it, the reader needs to bear in mind that although the scene is set on the eve of World War II, *The Cardinal* was published in the early Cold War years and reflects American Catholic thinking not just about a former menace, Hitler and the Nazis in 1939, but, to a still larger extent, about Joseph Stalin and the Soviet Union in 1950. As such, it constitutes an extraordinary vision both of the providentially assigned role of the United States in the world and also of the role of the Catholic Church as America's collaborator in the great struggle to uphold Western values.

Late at night Stephen Cardinal Fermoyle stands on the deck of an ocean liner—a British vessel, be it noted—as it ploughs bravely through the dark waters of the North Atlantic on its way to America. Fermoyle is a man with a mission, given him by no less than his old friend Pope Pius XII: to serve as a special wartime liaison between the pope and President Roosevelt, working in this momentous world crisis on behalf of the converging interests of the United States and the Church. As Fermoyle reflects on the international scene, the staunch British ship weaves its danger-laden way among menacing icebergs— threats from the north symbolizing Nazi Germany and the Communist U.S.S.R.

Here then are the imagined reflections on the Catholic Church and its role in the world as seen by "an American Cardinal, approaching the shores of his homeland" on the eve of the Second World War:

> Of necessity this visible organization must work within the existing pattern of society. It was legitimate therefore, by means of concordats and other diplomatic measures, to arrive at agreements with civil governments that recognized the rights of God and the claims of Christian conscience. But with powers that did *not* recognize these rights—with governments that exalted the State or any individual leader above God—no intercourse was possible. They were the enemy, the Dark Adversary wandering through the world, seeking the ruin of souls. Now more than ever it was imperative that the Church make common cause with those governments that recognized the right of worship and the primacy of God in men's lives.[3]

It is easy to imagine how powerfully such rhetoric must have resonated in the hearts of patriotic American Catholics confronting the Soviet menace as the Cold War began to heat up.

Francis Spellman's wartime services to his government and his Church weren't quite as dramatic as Stephen Fermoyle's, but they were impressive just the same. In January 1943, with Roosevelt's permission and American government help, Archbishop Spellman was preparing for the first of what would be a series of annual trips to visit American servicemen serving overseas, when, at a White House meeting, Roosevelt gave him an additional

[3] Robinson, *The Cardinal*, 509.

mission. Its nature became clear on February 12, when he met in Madrid with Spanish dictator Francisco Franco, as Roosevelt had asked him to do, and set out America's wartime aims. The session was credited with helping to ensure Spanish neutrality for the duration of the war.

This remarkable trip—reminiscent of the mission of Archbishop John Hughes to Europe on behalf of the Union during the Civil War—extended until July and also included stops at the Vatican and in North Africa, the Middle East, and the Holy Land. In London Archbishop Spellman lunched with Winston Churchill and his wife. In Rome he appears to have met with high-ranking officials of the Italian government. In Istanbul in May he made the acquaintance of the apostolic delegate, Archbishop Angelo Roncalli—later, Pope John XXIII. Returning to the United States, he urged Roosevelt in several White House meetings to treat Rome as an "open city" and refrain from bombing it—a plea that had only partial success.

In 1944 he was sounded out about becoming Vatican secretary of state, but he was indifferent to the offer and remained in New York. During the war, Pope Pius named no new cardinals, so it was hardly a surprise when Archbishop Spellman was one of the first postwar batch, elevated to the College of Cardinals at a consistory on February 18, 1946.

In the years that followed, he was active on numerous fronts. As a champion of anti-Communism, he was an early supporter of Senator Joseph McCarthy's efforts to out Communists who held or had held government posts. (Following McCarthy's largely self-inflicted fall, he privately extended a helping hand to the senator and his family.) A vocal foe of anti-Catholicism, he had a well-publicized falling-out with Eleanor Roosevelt, the president's widow, over aid to parochial schools. He worked for U.S.-Vatican diplomatic relations, although these were not destined to become reality until 1984 under President Ronald Reagan.

At the Second Vatican Council (1962–1965), Cardinal Spellman, a theological conservative, supported ecumenism on pragmatic grounds. Upon learning that Father John Courtney Murray, S.J., the American theologian of church-state relations, had not been invited to the council's first session, the cardinal took the priest to Rome with him as an advisor when the second session began. Murray thereafter was active in shaping Vatican II's document on religious liberty, which Spellman and the other Americans backed.

The cardinal was a prominent presence throughout the council, calling for retaining Latin in the Mass during the debate on the liturgy and strongly endorsing the draft of the Pastoral Constitution on the Church in the Modern World, *Gaudium et Spes*. Yet even before the council ended, younger bishops more in tune with Vatican II and the new times it ushered in had begun to emerge as leaders of the American hierarchy, while in the immediate postconciliar years it became increasingly clear that Francis Spellman's day was passing.

In December 1965, during an overseas trip to visit the troops, he borrowed the words of Stephen Decatur to declare his support for U.S. involvement in Vietnam: "My country, may it always be right, but right or wrong, my country." Back home, though, the war had already started to become unpopular, and the criticism of Spellman's remark ranged from pointed to vicious. He died in New York on December 2, 1967.

Historian Father Gerald P. Fogarty, S.J., writes that "American and Roman were the attributes of [Cardinal Spellman's] career as the most influential American

Catholic prelate of his age." No one has captured that complex reality better than Henry Morton Robinson in *The Cardinal*. At a crucial point in the novel, Stephen Fermoyle's dual loyalty to Rome and to America is challenged by a skeptical churchman. Fermoyle's subsequent soul searching has this result: "After months of intense and disciplined study, Stephen came to the private conclusion that the democratic idea with its emphasis on tolerance and individualism was the most hopeful manifestation of Christ's spirit in human affairs. And despite [his critic's] opinion to the contrary, Stephen continued to believe that the American phenomenon of a free Church in a free State had produced a Catholicism as stanch, loyal, and vigorous as any that preceded it."[4]

It is reasonable to think that Isaac Hecker, James Gibbons, and especially Francis Spellman would all have said amen to that.

[4] Robinson, *The Cardinal*, 292.

ARCHBISHOP FULTON SHEEN
(1895–1979)

Evangelist of the American Way

For several years during America's post-World War II religious boom, a Catholic bishop was the nation's best known and most popular preacher. Already famous as a writer and speaker, Fulton Sheen, starting in 1952, adroitly employed the new medium of television as a powerful electronic pulpit for the proclamation of the gospel, entering weekly into millions of American households to speak to Americans, Catholic and non-Catholic alike, of God and the meaning of man's existence. In this and other ways, Sheen became a larger-than-life embodiment of the virtues—and sometimes also the blemishes—of American Catholicism in the era of its ascendancy.

Bishop (eventually, Archbishop) Sheen stands with Protestant preachers like Billy Graham and Norman Vincent Peale as one of the most successful evangelists in the American manner during the middle years of the twentieth century. When *Time* magazine featured him on its cover in 1952, it called him simply "perhaps the most famous preacher in the U.S., certainly America's best-known Roman Catholic priest, and the newest star of U.S. television".[1]

[1] "Bishop Fulton Sheen: The First 'Televangelist'", *Time*, April 14, 1952.

96

He was many things to many people. Jewish sociologist of religion Will Herberg may have come closest to the mark when he wrote of Sheen as the preeminent Catholic representative of the tripartite Americanization of American religion that Herberg dubbed famously "Protestant, Catholic, Jew." In Sheen's peak years, he noted, the Catholic Church "finally arrived in America, emerging from its former status as a *foreign church* to join the national consensus as one of the three versions of the 'American Way of Life'."[2]

He was born May 8, 1895, in El Paso, Illinois, the eldest of four sons of Newton and Delia Sheen, and was baptized Peter John.[3] From the start, however, he was called "Fulton", his mother's maiden name. The family moved to nearby Peoria, Illinois, where Fulton served as an altar boy at St. Mary's Cathedral and was valedictorian at his graduation from Spalding Institute. From there he studied at St. Viator College in Illinois and St. Paul Seminary in Minnesota before his ordination as a priest on September 20, 1919. Following ordination, he did graduate studies at the Catholic University of America in Washington; the Catholic University of Louvain, Belgium; and the Pontifical University of St. Thomas Aquinas—the Angelicum—in Rome. In the end, he held doctorates in both philosophy and theology, and at Louvain received the Cardinal Mercier Prize for philosophy,

[2] For Herberg's development of his argument, see "Religion and Culture in Present-Day America", *Roman Catholicism and the American Way of Life*, ed. Thomas T. McAvoy, C.S.C. (Notre Dame, Ind.: University of Notre Dame Press, 1960), 4–19.

[3] Biographical information about Archbishop Sheen is drawn largely from Thomas C. Reeves, *America's Bishop: The Life and Times of Fulton J. Sheen* (San Francisco: Encounter Books, 2001). See also Mark S. Massa, *Catholics and American Culture* (New York: Crossroad, 1999), 82–101. Unless otherwise noted, Bishop Sheen quotations are from Reeves.

the first American to receive this prestigious honor. Returning to the United States in 1925, he did pastoral work in Peoria before going to the Catholic University of America, where he was to teach theology and later philosophy until 1950. His first book, a study in the spirit of Aquinas called *God and Intelligence in Modern Philosophy*, appeared in 1926.

The young professor had already begun to acquire a reputation as a speaker and writer when a new, highly significant opportunity came. In early 1930 the National Council of Catholic Men invited him to inaugurate a new series of Sunday evening talks called *The Catholic Hour*. Sheen obliged, speaking weekly from March 9 to April 30. Listener response was strongly positive, and in a short time he was the program's regular Sunday night speaker. In the first year alone, requests for transcripts of his weekly talks numbered as many as 163,800. The audience grew correspondingly, rising in time to four million listeners. *The Catholic Hour* in its prime drew as many as six thousand letters each week, with one in three of them from non-Catholics. In its first ten years, the program spread from twenty-two to ninety-five radio stations, and 1.75 million transcripts were mailed out. In 1946 *Time* spoke of "the golden-voiced Msgr. Fulton J. Sheen, U.S. Catholicism's famed proselytizer".

All the same, Sheen's career as a radio speaker pales by comparison with what he achieved on television. Though still in many ways in its infancy, television by the early 1950s had already become the nation's dominant broadcast medium. In 1952, the Dumont Network, smallest and weakest of the TV networks, decided to offer a weekly Tuesday night religious program in the first half hour of the 8 P.M.–9 P.M. time slot that then was ruled by comedian Milton Berle's hour-long show on another network. Dumont's religious offering was regarded as a virtual throwaway meant mainly to win good will for the network.

Sheen had been named an auxiliary bishop of New York the previous year. Now he agreed to give a weekly TV talk in the manner of his radio show, for which Dumont paid him $26,000 per program (all of the money went to charity). The series was called *Life Is Worth Living*, and the first show aired live from the stage of a New York theater on February 12, 1952. Elegantly attired in his picturesque episcopal robes and using neither teleprompter nor notes, the bishop wowed 'em.

By April he was receiving up to eighty-five hundred letters a week. In time, requests to the network for tickets to the theater where the program originated ran as high as five thousand weekly. Bishop Sheen received an Emmy for what a *New York Times* TV critic called "a remarkably absorbing half-hour of television". *Time* hailed him as "the first 'televangelist'". Accepting his Emmy, he paid tribute to "my four writers—Matthew, Mark, Luke and John". In 1955, the series, by now on ABC, peaked at thirty million viewers weekly. It remained on the air until 1957.

One of his most noted broadcasts was in February 1953. In it, the speaker denounced the regime of Soviet dictator Joseph Stalin and read the burial scene from Shakespeare's *Julius Caesar*, substituting the names of Stalin and his henchmen for the Roman figures of the play. "Stalin must one day meet his judgment," Bishop Sheen declared. Within a week, Stalin suffered a stroke and died.

Along with television and speaking appearances, Sheen kept up his output of popular books, eventually publishing seventy-three of them. Many are still in print. Among the titles are *Communism and the Conscience of the West, Peace of Soul, Three to Get Married*, and *Life Is Worth Living*, a series of volumes collecting his TV talks (1953–1957).[4] He also was famous for his celebrity converts, among them writer Heywood Broun; playwright, member of congress, and diplomat Clare Boothe Luce; Louis Budenz, former editor of the *Daily Worker*; musician Fritz Kreisler; and actress Virginia Mayo.

Sheen's anti-Communism antedated the 1953 Stalin broadcast by many years. Speaking in 1935 to a crowd of forty-three thousand in a Cleveland stadium, he declared: "In the future there will be only two great capitals in the world, Rome and Moscow; only two temples, the Kremlin and St. Peter's ... but there will be only one victory—if Christ wins, we win, and Christ cannot lose." But although anti-Communism made him a Cold War stalwart, he later opposed the Vietnam War.

Along with being named auxiliary bishop of New York, the Vatican had appointed Sheen national director of the Society for the Propagation of the Faith, an agency engaged in fundraising for the Church's foreign missions; in his sixteen years as director, it brought in some $200 million for evangelization overseas. In his capacity as director of Propagation of the Faith, however, he and Cardinal Spellman, with whom his relations already were strained, had a major falling-out. The immediate issue involved the allocation of Propagation funds, but its existential context was a deeply rooted personality clash between two men with large egos, each accustomed to having his way.

In October 1966 Pope Paul VI appointed him bishop of Rochester, New York. Sheen, by then seventy-one years of age, went there determined to carry out the reforms of

[4] *Communism and the Conscience of the West* (Indianapolis: Bobbs-Merrill, 1948); *Peace of Soul* (New York: Whittlesey House, 1949); *Three to Get Married* (New York: Appleton-Century-Crofts, 1951).

the recently concluded Second Vatican Council. But as a diocesan bishop he was not a success and was accused of failing to consult and practicing unilateral decision making. Asked later by an interviewer what went wrong in Rochester, he said simply: "I was never given a chance to administer a diocese before. I am a man of ideas. I have been thinking these problems through for many years; this was the first opportunity that I had to implement them." The Vatican announced his retirement as ordinary in mid-October 1969. He was named an archbishop and given a titular see.

Retirement for Sheen didn't mean slowing down, and he kept up a crowded schedule of speaking engagements and writing. When Pope John Paul II visited St. Patrick's Cathedral on October 2, 1979, Archbishop Sheen was among those greeting him. Reeves describes the dramatic scene: "When the new Pope made his entrance, the archbishop, led by his secretary and appearing 'feeble' ... made his way to the Holy Father in the sanctuary. Fulton fell to his knees. The Pope helped him to his feet, and the two men warmly embraced, amid thundering applause." Asked later what John Paul had said to him, Sheen answered, "He told me that I had written and spoken well of the Lord Jesus, and that I was a loyal son of the Church."

His last big writing project, published after his death, was his autobiography, *Treasure in Clay*. There he expressed regret for his failings, his vanity, and his comfortable life style. "I consider everything a waste except knowing Christ," Sheen wrote. "Anything that is done or read or spoken or enjoyed or suffered that does not bring me close to Him makes me ask myself: why all this waste?" On December 9, 1979, he was found before the Blessed Sacrament in his private chapel, dead of heart disease.

The process that could lead to Sheen's formal recognition as a saint was begun in 2002 and was said to be making good progress when, in 2014, a dispute between the Diocese of Peoria and the Archdiocese of New York over where his remains should be buried caused the Vatican to shelve the proceedings. At this time, admirers are hopeful the cause will soon be revived. Meanwhile he has the title "Servant of God".

In an essay on the entry of Catholics in America's cultural mainstream, Mark Massa, S.J., of Boston College, borrowing from the American Protestant theologian Reinhold Niebuhr, remarks that Sheen's huge popular success was a noteworthy illustration of the abandonment of the "Christ above Culture" model characteristic of immigrant Catholicism, according to which the Church stood above the secular culture in judgment, and its replacement by a "Christ and Culture" model in which assimilated Catholics blended into the surrounding milieu and adopted its values. The "paradox" of Fulton Sheen, Father Massa maintains, was that although he personally held to the older model, his hugely successful venture into network television reinforced the newer one.

"Quite paradoxically," Massa writes,

> Bishop Fulton J. Sheen's *Life Is Worth Living* both abetted and announced the "arrival" of Catholics into the American cultural mainstream, but with a model of "Christ and Culture" he would have disdained and with a resulting relationship with the Catholic tradition that would have worried him.... One might fruitfully wonder what Sheen would have made of the "uses" his media popularity provided for American Catholics seemingly more worried about the "American" than "Catholic"

part of their identities in discerning how and why life was worth living.[5]

On the whole, that seems about right.

Still, Sheen himself never wavered in his certainty that Catholicism held the answers to just about everything. He once told a television interviewer, "I'm never haunted by doubts about essentials.... No, as regards the gospel and Christ and the Church I have a certitude that is absolute. About other things, I don't care so much." Sheen biographer Thomas Reeves writes that this attitude goes a long way to account for his "lack of appeal" to today's intellectuals, yet it may also be that his certitude best explains his continuing hold on an audience of devoted readers and listeners who still turn to his books and broadcast talks as a source of inspiration, enlightenment, and especially certainty.

An experience of mine not long ago suggests something of the sort. During a retreat I was treated to Sheen audiotapes played as spiritual reading at meals. As I listened with interest and a bit of nostalgia to that famous voice—supple, resonant, often throbbing with intensity—and imagined the piercing gaze of the speaker's deep-set eyes, I couldn't help thinking that this was too obviously a performance, sincere yet also calculated for effect, and that in the end the manner was a distraction from what Sheen had to say. A casual style featuring simplicity and spontaneity—or at least what can pass for them—today appears to be the norm for nearly every kind of public utterance, from sermons to campaign speeches. By contrast, Fulton Sheen's high-octane rhetoric and histrionic style make him a period piece.

---

[5] Massa, *Catholics and American Culture*, 101.

Even so, he has an important lesson for would-be evangelizers of the present day. His permanent power is neither his message nor his style but the obvious, moving fact that he believed so intensely in the gospel that he preached. Faith, not old-time eloquence, is Archbishop Sheen's legacy to evangelization and evangelizers.

JOHN F. KENNEDY
(1917–1963)

Rome Meets Camelot

Disagreement runs deep about John F. Kennedy's place in American history and especially in the history of the Catholic Church in the United States. Whatever position anyone holds on those questions, however, it's obvious that his tragic death and the meaning of his glamorous but troubled life both carry heavy symbolic and emotional weight with Catholics.

And with good reason, for John F. Kennedy remains an enormously popular figure. For Catholics in particular, his ascent to the highest office in the land heralded the removal of an ancient stain along with the realization of a dream that long seemed out of reach, while his death by an assassin's bullet barely three years after his election took on something like the aura of martyrdom.

Since Kennedy's death, the Camelot image of JFK, his family and entourage, and the Kennedy years in general has become entrenched in popular mythology. Among American presidents, Kennedy occupies the topmost ranks on the popularity scale, and his photogenic wife, children, and siblings continue to be objects of intense interest and passionate devotion. Although historians rate Kennedy a fair to middling president at best, the Camelot version of his brief presidency (1961–1963) is that this was a golden age of extraordinary achievement cut short by untimely death.

John Fitzgerald Kennedy was born May 29, 1917, the second of four sons of Joseph P. and Rose Fitzgerald Kennedy.[1] Father and mother both were from politically prominent Irish American families, and Rose Kennedy's father, "Honey Fitz" Fitzgerald, had been mayor of Boston.

Growing up deeply resentful of the anti-Irish, anti-Catholic prejudice he encountered among Boston's WASP (White Anglo Saxon Protestant) elite, Joe Kennedy had made a fortune as an investor and corporate wheeler and dealer. *Fortune* ranked him among the top twenty wealthiest Americans. He also became an influential figure in Democratic politics, serving as President Franklin Roosevelt's first chairman of the Securities and Exchange Commission and as ambassador to Great Britain. But his comments in a 1940 interview at the height of the Battle of Britain ("democracy is finished in England") ended not only his ambassadorial career but whatever hopes he entertained of becoming president himself. His political ambitions thereafter focused on his sons, and after the eldest, Joseph Jr., a Navy pilot, was killed in action in 1944, that meant second son Jack.

During the war, JFK commanded torpedo boats in the South Pacific, earning high marks for bravery by rescuing crew members after his boat was sunk. In 1946 he was elected to the House of Representatives and in 1952 to the Senate. In 1956 he battled Senator Estes Kefauver of Arkansas for a place on the Democratic ticket as Adlai Stevenson's running mate. Kennedy lost, but his strong

---

[1] Biographical information about Kennedy is drawn largely from Richard Reeves, *President Kennedy: Profile of Power* (New York: Simon and Schuster, 1994). John F. Kennedy quotations are from this source unless otherwise noted. See also William B. Prendergast, *The Catholic Voter in American Politics: The Passing of the Democratic Monolith* (Washington: Georgetown University Press, 1999), 135–48.

performance put him in the front ranks of likely contenders for the Democratic presidential nomination four years later. In 1957, his book *Profiles in Courage*, about eight senators ranging from John Quincy Adams to Robert A. Taft, received the Pulitzer Prize for biography (it appears that much of the writing was done by speechwriter and close friend Theodore Sorensen).[2]

As Kennedy and his advisors surveyed the scene while contemplating a run for president, he had two strikes against him from the start. One was the idea that Joe Kennedy was trying to buy the election for his son. The other, especially alarming in light of Al Smith's crushing defeat in 1928, was the fact that he was a Catholic.

There was little to be done about the first, since the senior Kennedy did indeed bankroll his son's political career to the hilt. As for the second, political scientists at the University of Michigan later concluded that the religious issue really was the strongest single factor in the presidential election of 1960. Nationally, JFK lost 6.5 percent of the votes of Protestant Democrats and independents because he was a Catholic, along with a whopping 17.2 percent of the Southern vote. As compensation, however, he was supported by 80 percent of the Catholics who voted. The result was a razor-thin victory over Richard Nixon and the Republicans. Joe Kennedy, by that time crippled by a debilitating stroke, thought Catholic support should have been higher and blamed the American bishops, except for Cardinal Cushing of Boston, for not turning out more Catholics to vote for his son.

The years of the Kennedy presidency were crowded with drama. JFK projected a public image of youth, vigor,

[2]John F. Kennedy, *Profiles in Courage* (New York: Harper and Brothers, 1955).

and dynamic leadership that inspired an upsurge of idealism among young and not-so-young Americans, with the enthusiastic reception of the Peace Corps perhaps its most visible expression. Idealism would soon evaporate in the face of America's growing involvement in Vietnam, but for as long as it lasted it redounded powerfully to Kennedy's advantage. People sometimes spoke effusively of the "two Johns"—Kennedy and Pope John XXIII, the much-loved pope of Vatican Council II who died less than six months before the American president.

On matters of substance, nonetheless, the Kennedy record was mixed. Summing up the thirty-fifth president in his book *President Kennedy: Profile of Power*, historian Richard Reeves describes him as "a gifted professional politician reacting to events he often neither foresaw nor understood, handling some well, others badly, but always ready with plausible explanations".

In the international field, his administration got off to a rocky start with the badly planned and ill-fated Bay of Pigs invasion of Cuba in April 1961. Engineered by the CIA and okayed by Kennedy, this was an attempt by Cuban exiles to overthrow the Fidel Castro regime; but without the American air cover the invasion force apparently expected, it was quickly overwhelmed by the Cuban military. Besides leaving the United States with a black eye, the fiasco fostered an impression of fecklessness and inexperience on the part of the president and his people.

Things lurched further downhill at a summit meeting in Vienna between Kennedy and Soviet Premier Nikita Khrushchev. The Russian leader was aggressive and bullying, and treated the American president with something very like contempt. Kennedy told *New York Times* Washington bureau chief James Reston that the encounter had been the "worst thing in my life", adding, "He thinks because of the Bay of Pigs that I'm inexperienced.

Probably thinks I'm stupid. Maybe most important, he thinks that I had no guts."

The U.S.-Soviet relationship hit rock bottom in October 1962, when Khrushchev, apparently emboldened by his perception of Kennedy as weak, sought to gain strategic advantage in the struggle with America by placing nuclear missiles in Cuba. Kennedy responded with a naval blockade and declared his intention to intercept the Russian ships that were carrying the weapons. The world teetered on the brink of nuclear war until Pope John and others helped broker a deal under which the ships turned back while the United States agreed to pull some obsolescent U.S. missiles out of Turkey.

It was hardly all sweetness and light between the United States and the Soviets thereafter, but in July 1963 the two powers, after years of maneuvering and posturing, did at least manage to agree on a limited nuclear test ban treaty. This may have been John Kennedy's greatest foreign policy achievement.

On the domestic front, far and away the biggest issue of the Kennedy years was the campaign for African American civil rights led by Dr. Martin Luther King Jr. Though genuinely supportive, the president was also fearful of alienating Southern segregationists who played a large role in the Democratic Party. At a White House meeting not long before the famous March on Washington in August 1963, he was cool to the idea and cautioned King against "the wrong kind of demonstration at the wrong time".

Like many holders of America's highest office before and since, Kennedy presented a public face that often failed to match reality. That was true, for instance, where his health was concerned. Asked if he had Addison's disease, a potentially terminal failure of the adrenal gland, he said flatly, "I never had Addison's disease." But he did. According to Reeves, Kennedy received the last rites of the Church at least four times as an adult and was "something of a medical marvel, kept alive by complicated daily combinations of pills and injections".

So also of his relations with women. Like his father, JFK was a womanizer who, despite his image as a devoted husband and father, was serially unfaithful to his wife. Before a 1963 audience at the Vatican with Pope Paul VI, he passed the night in a commandeered villa with a woman who'd been brought in for the occasion. Next day he and the pope spent the eighteen minutes of their meeting talking about world peace.

Kennedy and Catholicism is a special topic that deserves special attention. Although he had been raised as a Catholic, John Kennedy received, as he later said, a thoroughly secular education "from the elementary grades to Harvard". Not surprisingly, his religious knowledge was scanty and superficial. Yet on January 20, 1961, he concluded his inaugural address with these ringing words: "With a good conscience our only sure reward, with history the final judge of our deeds, let us go forth to lead the land we love, asking His blessing and His help, but knowing that here on earth God's work must truly be our own." Whether JFK wrote that or Ted Sorenson or somebody else, the fact remains that John Kennedy spoke the words with the nation and the world watching and listening, and he deserves credit for that.

During his time in the White House, however, Kennedy was careful to avoid confrontations about his religion and took stands opposed to official Church views on things like aid to parochial schools and American diplomatic recognition of Communist-ruled Yugoslavia. Few Catholics raised objections. To a considerable extent, the religious issue had been worked out during the 1960 presidential campaign, and what the president did later was essentially what he'd said he would do.

In fact, Kennedy had signaled what that would be in a *Look* magazine interview well before the campaign. "His theme is that religion is personal, politics are public, and the twain need never meet and conflict," interviewer Fletcher Knebel, a well-known journalist of the day, summed up. Reactions in the Catholic press were largely negative. "To relegate your conscience to your 'private life' is not only unrealistic, but dangerous as well," said *Ave Maria*, a Catholic weekly published at Notre Dame.

But the question of Kennedy's religion would not go away, and once the campaign began, the Catholic issue heated up rapidly, coming to a boil in early September 1960. A hundred and fifty Protestant leaders headed by Dr. Norman Vincent Peale, a popular preacher and author of the best-selling *The Power of Positive Thinking*, demonstrated their capacity for thinking negatively by issuing a statement that called the Catholic Church a "political organization" and declared that neither Kennedy nor any other Catholic would be able to "withstand the determined efforts of the hierarchy to work its will in American political life".

The candidate moved quickly to respond. On September 12, speaking to an audience of ministers in Houston, Kennedy delivered one of the most important speeches of his career—arguably, indeed, one of the most important American political manifestoes of the twentieth century. Its aim was to disarm suspicion that he would be influenced by his religious faith in performing the duties of president. On the crucial subject of conscience, he said: "Whatever issue may come before me as president—on birth control, divorce, censorship, gambling or any other subject—I will make my decision ... in accordance with what my conscience tells me to be in the national interest, and without regard to outside religious pressures or dictates."

The relationship between faith and politics is admittedly complex. While no one expects politicians in a pluralistic democracy to translate doctrine into law, neither can religious believers turn their backs on their faith-based convictions about right and wrong. Rather, the conscientious believer filters those convictions through the prism of prudence (the virtue that guides the "art of the possible" that politics is) in order to reach practical conclusions about what can and should be done in light of moral norms and the standards of conduct appropriate to a democratic polity.

By contrast, Kennedy's words were an unconditional affirmation of the supremacy of autonomous individual conscience over any other source of moral guidance. Father John Courtney Murray, S.J., the preeminent American Catholic theologian on questions of church and state, later called the position that "I have a right to do what my conscience tells me to do, simply because my conscience tells me to do it" a "perilous theory" that, contrary to the teaching of the Second Vatican Council, ends in "subjectivism".[3]

Many Catholic politicians have followed the path marked out by JFK in Houston. Catholic officeholders and candidates who lend support to causes like legalized abortion and same-sex marriage are in effect following his lead. Now as then, however, the issue isn't taking orders from the pope and the bishops—something those supposedly power-hungry ecclesiastics neither expect nor want—but how to apply moral principles grounded in faith to real-world politics. John Kennedy's innovative and influential approach lay in giving assurances that he wouldn't even try. We are still living with the consequences.

[3]John Courtney Murray, S.J., footnote five to Declaration on Religious Freed (*Dignitatis Humanae*), *The Documents of Vatican II*, ed. Walter M. Abbott, S.J. (New York: The American Press, 1966), 679.

DOROTHY DAY
(1897–1980)

Catholicism as Countercultural

In one of those snarky stories about clerical life that were his specialty—it's called "The Forks"—the American Catholic writer J. F. Powers capsulized in a single, prickly sentence the edgy relationship between a stuffy, self-important pastor and his young, mildly progressive curate: "He found Father Eudex reading *The Catholic Worker* one day and had not trusted him since."[1]

There was a time when quite a few Catholics, not just stuffy pastors either, took much the same view of Dorothy Day and her companions—dangerous radicals, that is. "It's getting so you can't tell the Catholics from the Communists," Powers' Monsignor complains in *Forks*. Some people may feel the same way about Day even now. Yet the Church is looking into the possibility of declaring her a saint.

Day was cofounder of the Catholic Worker movement and longtime editor of its penny-a-copy newspaper of the same name. The gospel according to Dorothy was a heady mix of the inspiring and the infuriating. From the mid-1930s to the early 1980s she preached radical Christianity and social activism to a sometimes appreciative, sometimes puzzled, and sometimes outraged audience of

---

[1] "The Forks" in *The Stories of J. F. Powers* (New York: Review of Books, 2000), 93–110.

Catholics busy being good, patriotic free-market Americans. Historian Charles Morris says she "transformed the social conscience of a whole generation of young clergy".[2] To which one might add: lay intellectuals, writers, and journalists, too.

Now, slowly but apparently steadily, the effort to have her canonized is moving ahead. Yet this ex-Communist who had several love affairs and an abortion might not have entirely welcomed that. "Don't call me a saint," she famously said. "I don't want to be dismissed so easily."

Dorothy Day was born November 8, 1897, in Brooklyn.[3] A few years later, her father, a sportswriter, took a job with a San Francisco newspaper and moved the family there, but the San Francisco earthquake of 1906 wiped out the paper and, with it, the elder Day's job, and the family shifted to Chicago.

The parents had been married in an Episcopal ceremony but seldom went to church. Even so, Day's childhood was by no means lacking in religious sensibility. "We did not search for God when we were children. We took Him for granted," Day recalls in her autobiography. She also acquired a strong ethical sense—"a sense of right and wrong, good and evil". In Chicago her interest in religion grew and expanded, and she was baptized and confirmed in the Episcopal Church. Around this time, too, she received what she later called her "first impulse toward Catholicism"—the glimpse of a Catholic friend's mother kneeling in her bedroom at prayer. "For many a night after

[2] Morris, *American Catholic*, 141.

[3] Biographical information about Day is drawn largely from her autobiography, *The Long Loneliness* (New York: HarperCollins, 1997). Unless otherwise noted, Dorothy Day quotations are from this source. See also Charles R. Morris, *American Catholic* (New York: Times Books, 1997), 141–45, and Mark S. Massa, *Catholics and American Culture* (New York: Crossroad, 1999), 102–27.

that," Day writes, "I used to plague my sister with my long prayers.... So we began to practice being saints—it was a game with us."

As she moved into her midteens, however, the girl began to have doubts about religion. On the one hand, she saw churchgoers who were well-off. On the other hand, she saw the poor. "I did not see anyone taking off his coat and giving it to the poor. I didn't see anyone having a banquet and calling in the lame, the halt and the blind." At the University of Illinois, Day joined the Socialist Party. "The Marxist slogan, 'Workers of the world, unite! You have nothing to lose but your chains,' seemed to me a most stirring battle cry."

Leaving the university after two years, she headed back to New York, where she wrote for Socialist publications, was active in radical causes, including feminism and free love, and pursued a Bohemian lifestyle in the company of artists and activists. In 1917 she was arrested for picketing for women's suffrage at the White House and spent fifteen days in jail, where she and her companions went on a hunger strike. For reasons unknown, Day asked for a Bible. Eventually she was given one. "I read it with the sense of coming back to something of my childhood that I had lost," she recalled. "My heart swelled with joy and thankfulness for the Psalms. The man who sang these songs knew sorrow and expected joy."

Her intimates in these years included playwright Eugene O'Neill and prominent Communists, with one of whom she had an affair. After still another affair, around 1920 or 1921, she had an abortion. Thereafter she married briefly, published a semiautobiographical novel whose screen rights she sold to Hollywood for $2,500, and bought herself a Staten Island beach cottage where she lived from 1925 to 1929 with a man named Forster.

In 1926 Day gave birth to a daughter, whom she named Tamar. Now her old interest in Catholicism not only revived but intensified. She met a nun named Sister Aloysia, discussed religion with her, had her baby baptized Teresa, and studied the faith. On December 28, 1927, Day was received into the Catholic Church, with Sister Aloysia as her sponsor. Forster resented her new religious interests and, when Dorothy persisted, walked out for good.

"God always gives us a chance to show our preference for him," she later reflected. "With me it was to give up my ... life with Forster. You do these things blindly, not because it is your natural inclination—you are going against nature when you do them—but because you wish to live in conformity with the will of God."

Conforming to God's will had now become a matter of central concern to Dorothy, but that didn't mean abandoning old convictions about a just social order. Instead, finding and living a practical synthesis between faith and radical social causes was an increasingly urgent concern.

The turning point came early in the Great Depression. Working as a journalist, Day covered a jobs demonstration in Washington that had been organized by Communists. As she watched the demonstrators, she thought: "How little, how puny my work had been since becoming a Catholic.... How self-centered, how ingrown, how lacking in sense of community!" After the demonstration, Day went to the National Shrine of the Immaculate Conception, and, kneeling there in the shadowy crypt church, she offered "a special prayer, a prayer which came with tears and anguish, that some way would open for me to use what talents I possessed for my fellow workers, for the poor".

Returning to New York, she found waiting for her a somewhat disheveled French peasant "as ragged and rugged as any of the marchers I had left", who was also a radical Catholic and a self-taught social thinker. His name was Peter Maurin. He had been referred to Day by a Catholic editor, and he wanted to share with her his vision of a new movement and a new way of life. Later she recalled:

> Peter rejoiced to see men do great things and dream great dreams. He wanted them to stretch out their arms to their brothers, because he knew that the surest way to find God, to find the good, was through one's brothers.... I can well recognize the fact that people remaining as they are, Peter's program is impossible. But it would become actual, given a people changed in heart and mind, so that they would observe the new commandment of love, or desire to.

The Catholic Worker movement had been born.

With Day as editor, the first issue of *The Catholic Worker* newspaper appeared on May 1, 1933. It aimed to be an alternative to the Communist *Daily Worker*. That first issue asked: "Is it not possible to be radical and not atheist?" For the next half century Day worked hard to show it could be done.

During the Spanish Civil War, she opposed the Nationalist side and General Franco, whom most Catholics supported in opposition to the leftist Spanish Republicans. She was an uncompromising pacifist, a position that cost the Catholic Worker members and support during World War II. "We love our country and we love our President," Day wrote after the United States entered the war. But even so, "we are still pacifists. Our manifesto is the Sermon on the Mount." When the United States dropped the first atomic bombs on Hiroshima and Nagasaki in 1945, Day's was one of the few Catholic voices raised in public protest. She supported the labor movement, racial justice, and the California farm workers led by Cesar Chavez.

In the early Cold War years, Day marched uncompromisingly to a drummer very different from the one heeded by most of her coreligionists in the United States. This was the era when Henry Morton Robinson's best seller *The Cardinal*, loosely based on the career of Cardinal Spellman of New York, depicted a heroic churchman whom the pope chose as his emissary to the American president in forging a de facto alliance of church and state as a bulwark against Soviet Communism. The idea resonated with most American Catholics. But Day joined other pacifists in peace demonstrations and for her trouble now and then served time in jail. She praised Fidel Castro's social revolution in Cuba while deploring its antireligious policies. A few years later, she opposed the Vietnam War. While calling the Christmas season visits by Cardinal Spellman to American troops overseas "brave", she also wrote: "What are all those Americans doing all over the world so far from our own shores?"

Day was intensely loyal to Church teaching but had no hesitation about challenging Church leaders when she thought they were wrong. In 1949, she criticized Cardinal Spellman during a grave diggers' strike at New York Catholic cemeteries for bringing in seminarians to substitute for the striking workers. (The cardinal, for his part, saw Communist influence in the workers' union.) In 1951, the archdiocese told the *Catholic Worker* either to stop publishing or remove the word "Catholic" from its name. Day did neither, and the archdiocese dropped the matter.

Though never large in numbers, the Catholic Worker movement over the years came to have houses of hospitality in a number of cities as well as a Catholic Worker farm. Day herself lived in a Catholic Worker house in New York, and it was there that she died, of a heart attack, on

November 29, 1980. Of the movement she helped create and led, she wrote in *The Long Loneliness*:

> The most significant thing about the Catholic Worker is poverty, some say.
> The most significant thing is community, others say. We are not alone any more.
> But the final word is love. At times it has been ... a harsh and dreadful thing, and our very faith in love has been tried through fire.
> We cannot love God unless we love each other, and to love we must know each other. We know Him in the breaking of the bread, and we know each other in the breaking of the bread, and we are not alone any more. Heaven is a banquet and life is a banquet, too, even with a crust, where there is companionship.
> We have all known the long loneliness and we have learned that the only solution is love and that love comes with community.

The first steps toward her possible beatification and canonization were taken in 2000 by the late John Cardinal O'Connor of New York, and the efforts have continued under Timothy Cardinal Dolan. At his urging, the U.S. bishops in November 2012 voted to endorse her cause. The cardinal called her "a saint for our time".[4]

But saints often make people uncomfortable, and Day clearly did her share of that. Whether she was inexcusably naïve about Communism is, and probably will remain, in dispute. While remaining a lifelong admirer of the idealistic Communists who had once been her friends, she criticized the evil means often used by Communism to achieve its

[4]Sharon Otterman, "In Hero of the Catholic Left, a Conservative Cardinal Sees a Saint", *New York Times*, November 26, 2012.

ends. Many similarly think she should have showed more concern about the harm done by the self-indulgent hippie culture of the 1960s and 1970s.

Yet Dorothy Day has had a twofold influence on American Catholicism that is likely not only to endure but to become increasingly relevant as the Church's situation here becomes more difficult—something that seems all too likely to happen. First, she showed people a faith-based alternative to secular radicalism—a way to work for a culture of love rather than a secular utopia. Second, she lived a form of countercultural Catholicism at a time when assimilation into secular culture was assumed to be the correct path for American Catholics. Both lessons are important ones, but the second way of witnessing is especially needed now. In February 2013 Pope Benedict XVI said of her: "The journey towards faith in such a secularized environment was particularly difficult, but grace acts nonetheless."[5] As this is being written, she has the title "Servant of God".

[5] Wednesday audience catechesis, quoted in "Looking to Legacy, Pope Mentions Dorothy Day", *National Catholic Reporter*, February 13, 2013.

FATHER JOHN COURTNEY MURRAY (1904–1967)

We (Used To) Hold These Truths

By far the most sophisticated intellectual landmark of the project for the Americanization of American Catholicism is *We Hold These Truths: Catholic Reflections on the American Proposition*.[1] In this collection of essays, published in 1960, Father John Courtney Murray, S.J., deploys the resources of his much-loved natural law tradition and his own eloquence to celebrate and expound upon the compatibility of the Catholic Church and American liberal democracy. This theme had occupied the Americanist wing of the Church since the days of Isaac Hecker a century earlier, and Murray's book established him as the intellectual capstone of a line that extends from the founder of the Paulists and the Irish Americans who launched the Knights of Columbus to princes of the Church like Cardinal Gibbons of Baltimore and Cardinal Spellman of New York.

We Hold These Truths ends on this ringing note:

> If there is a law immanent in man—a dynamic, constructive force for rationality in human affairs, that works itself out, because it is a natural law, in spite of contravention

---

[1] John Courtney Murray, S.J., *We Hold These Truths: Catholic Reflections on the American Proposition* (New York: Sheed and Ward, 1960). Unless otherwise indicated, quotations are from this source.

by passion and evil and all the corruptions of power—one
may with sober reason believe in, and hope for, a future of
rational progress. And this belief and hope is strengthened
when one considers that this dynamic order of reason in
man ... has its origin and sanction in an eternal order of
reason whose fulfillment is the object of God's majestic will.

Here was John Courtney Murray's great vision for
America. Yet even as he wrote, he was painfully aware
that the time for its realization might by then have come
and gone. "The tradition of reason, which is known as
the natural law, is dead," he wrote. "The ethic which
launched Western constitutionalism and endured long
enough to give essential form to the American system of
government has now ceased to sustain the structure and
direct the action of this constitutional commonwealth."
Today, as critics point out, it would be difficult to say
what, if anything, has taken its place.[2]

John Courtney Murray was born September 12, 1904,
in New York and joined the New York province of the
Society of Jesus—the Jesuits—in 1920. After studying clas-
sics and philosophy at Boston College, he taught for three
years at a Jesuit school in Manila, then returned to the
United States and in 1933 was ordained a priest. Following
ordination, the Jesuits sent him to Rome to study theology
at the Gregorian University, where he received his doc-
torate in 1937. Next he was assigned to teach at the Jesuits'
seminary in Woodstock, Maryland. In 1941, he was given
the additional job of editing the Society's influential journal, *Theological Studies*. He held both positions until his
death of a heart attack in New York on August 16, 1967.

---

[2] See, for example, Alasdair MacIntyre, *After Virtue* (Notre Dame, Ind.: University of Notre Dame Press, 1981), and George Marsden, *The Twilight of the
American Enlightenment* (New York: Basic Books, 2014).

Church-state issues were much on Americans' minds in the late 1940s and 1950s, a time when the growing size and influence of the Catholic Church were reviving ancient suspicions in some quarters regarding Catholics' intentions if they should become the dominant religious and cultural body in the United States. These new tensions found expression in the founding of a group called Protestants and Other Americans United for Separation of Church and State (now, simply Americans United) as well as in Supreme Court decisions that raised a "wall of separation"—an expression not found in the Constitution—between government and religion. In 1949, a controversialist named Paul Blanshard published a volume provocatively titled *American Freedom and Catholic Power*, and Blanshard's broadside against the looming Catholic threat found a place on the best-seller list.

It was in this overheated cultural environment that Father Murray began writing on the church-state question and publishing the results in *Theological Studies* and the Jesuit weekly *America*. His views on church-state separation and government neutrality toward religion—even in countries where the majority of the population was Catholic—in time drew the attention of other, more traditional Catholic thinkers, especially Monsignor Joseph Fenton and Father Francis Connell, C.Ss.R, of the Catholic University of America and, eventually, Alfredo Cardinal Ottaviani, head of the Vatican's Holy Office, the predecessor of today's Congregation for the Doctrine of the Faith. In 1953 Monsignor Fenton's *American Ecclesiastical Review* published an article by Cardinal Ottaviani criticizing Murrray's ideas.

The priest's religious superiors now instructed him to seek the approval of Roman censors before publishing further on church and state; and in 1955 he was told to stop writing on the subject entirely. According to historian James Hitchcock, the silencing "seems mainly to have reflected the caution of his Jesuit superiors.... Murray's superiors correctly assessed the situation when they counseled that a prudent silence would eventually lead to a renewed recognition of his work."[3] In any case, just five years later *We Hold These Truths* made its appearance.

When the Second Vatican Council began in 1962, Father Murray was not invited; but Cardinal Spellman remedied that snub the following year at the council's second session, taking the priest with him to Rome as his *peritus* or theological advisor. From then on, the American theologian played a role in shaping Vatican II's groundbreaking declaration on religious liberty, *Dignitatis Humanae*, a much-debated document that the American bishops at the council strongly supported. Both Murray and the Vatican II declaration ground their argument for religious liberty not on subjective conscience but on the objective dignity of the human person. Seen in that light, the theologian believed, the American understanding of religious freedom and Catholic doctrine are entirely compatible.

John Courtney Murray is often linked with John F. Kennedy, and some profess to see the theologian's hand in the famous speech that Kennedy delivered in Houston in September 1960 to an audience of Protestant ministers. Coming at the height of that year's presidential campaign, in the midst of a flare-up of bigotry aimed at Kennedy's Catholicism that badly rattled the candidate and his advisors, it offered assurances that if he was elected president, he would not permit his faith to interfere with what he thought best for the country.

[3] James Hitchcock, "The Background of the Murray Thesis", in *We Hold These Truths and More: Further Catholic Reflections on the American Proposition*, ed. Donald J. D'Elia and Stephen M. Krason (Steubenville, Ohio: Franciscan University Press, 1993), 11.

Diverse claims have been made about Murray's role in the speech. People around Kennedy like Theodore Sorenson and Arthur Schlesinger Jr. suggested it was substantial, and Sorenson said he had telephoned the priest to get his approval of the text. Father Murray acknowledged that he and Sorenson had spoken but said he couldn't recall the substance of the conversation. Kennedy's position on church and state, he said, went further in separating the two than he himself preferred.

However that may be, soon after Kennedy's victory *Time* magazine featured the Jesuit on its cover. But he was no great fan of JFK. And in a commentary on *Dignitatis Humanae*, Murray underlined the obligations of Catholics to the teaching of the Church and declared the exaltation of subjective conscience to be a "perilous theory".[4]

Appearing in 1960, at one of the darkest moments of the Cold War, *We Hold These Truths* was in part a paean to the natural law tradition, grounded in Aristotle and later extensively developed by Catholic thinkers, which the book's author believed provided the conceptual foundation for America's struggle with Soviet Communism. As such, the volume represents a highly sophisticated Catholic voice amid a chorus of fierce anti-Communism that included such other notable Catholics as Cardinal Spellman, Archbishop Fulton Sheen, Senator Joseph McCarthy of Wisconsin, and President Kennedy himself.

But Murray's distinctive contribution had less to do with anti-Communism or any other issue specific to his day than with his ardent advocacy of natural law and his argument that this Catholic-inspired school of thinking had made an indispensable contribution to the thinking of the American founders in organizing the public order and

---

[4] See Murray's footnote 5 to *Dignitatis Humanae* in *The Documents of Vatican II*, ed. Walter M. Abbott, S.J. (New York: America Press, 1966), 679.

the conduct of human affairs in the nation's foundational documents. This linkage between the natural law tradition and American constitutionalism was, Murray believed, the essential basis of the compatibility of Catholicism and Americanism.

He was far too intelligent, however, to imagine that his enthusiasm for natural law was widely understood and shared by the intellectual and political elite of secular America. On the contrary, he wrote in *We Hold These Truths*, by that time "its [natural law's] dynamic had run out", replaced by a regrettable "impotence" to serve as a source of public policy. Where Americans had at one time consented to policies and laws because they embodied a moral tradition that they held in common, "today no such moral tradition lives among the American people ... the tradition of reason, which is known as the tradition of natural law, is dead."

But Murray did not despair. Convinced of the intrinsic, perennial power of natural law, he held that America had only to return to its eighteenth-century natural law roots in order once again to tap this source of intellectual and moral vigor. In comparison with competitors like Marxism, relativism, and "evolutionary scientific humanism", he wrote, "the doctrine of natural law offers a more profound metaphysic, a more integral humanism, a fuller rationality, a more complete philosophy of man in his nature and history."

Although Murray's account of natural law's role in the American founding has been dismissed by some critics as myth making, the central thrust of his argument has been shared and kept alive since his death by a group of American Catholic intellectuals who include Michael Novak, the late Father Richard John Neuhaus, George Weigel, and Robert George. In practical terms, their emphasis is

on restoring the basic principles of the American founding, including a social order grounded in the family and
religion and the body of moral principles that they espouse
and seek to instill.

A second group of Catholic thinkers, represented by
theologian David Schindler and philosopher Alasdair
MacIntyre, thinks otherwise. They reject the idea that
Catholicism and liberal democracy in its modern secular
form are fundamentally compatible, thanks to natural law,
arguing instead that contemporary liberalism is an expression of an individualistic conception of the human person
that gives rise to a correspondingly pluralistic and fractured
social order. As for the American founding, it is said, its
essential insights were drawn from deistic-agnostic thinkers of the eighteenth-century Enlightenment rather than
from Catholic natural law thinkers of the Middle Ages.

This argument is likely to continue. But regardless of
which side you take, there is no avoiding the fact that American secularism is today profoundly hostile to the Catholic
Church on a broad range of issues, from contraception and
abortion to the uniqueness and social indispensability of
man-woman marriage and the right conferred upon religious believers by the constitutional guarantee of religious
liberty to stand their ground in the face of secular pressure
to conform to the new secular dispensation.

From the perspective of faith, moreover, the tragedy
is that a large number of American Catholics—a substantial majority, to judge from poll numbers on sacramental
participation and Catholic opinion on a broad range of
moral and ecclesiastical questions—have adopted the
beliefs and values characteristic of American secularism. In
their preface to a collection of papers on Murray, Donald
J. D'Elia and Stephen M. Krason speak of the "substantial number of Catholic politicians who have announced

that the Church's teaching on such matters as abortion will not be allowed to influence their public posture or decisions. They have thus made it seem, contrary to the Murray thesis, that Catholic teaching and the natural law are completely out of the picture as far as American politics is concerned."[5]

Already in the 1950s John Courtney Murray saw these troubling realities beginning to take shape and sought to revivify a public consensus grounded in natural law in hopes of warding them off. The alternative, he believed, was "barbarism". He wrote:

> Society becomes barbaric when men are huddled together under the rule of force and fear; when economic interests assume the primacy over higher values; when material standards of mass and quantity crush out the values of quality and excellence; when technology assumes an autonomous existence and embarks on a course of unlimited self-exploitation without purposeful guidance from the higher disciplines of politics and morals ...; when the state reaches the paradoxical point of being everywhere intrusive and also impotent, possessed of immense power and powerless to achieve rational ends; when the ways of men come under the sway of the instinctual, the impulsive, the compulsive.
>
> When things like this happen, barbarism is abroad, whatever the surface impressions of urbanity. Men have ceased to live together according to reasonable laws.

Who doubts that barbarism is abroad in the land now?

Written on the cusp of a cultural revolution that was soon to sweep aside so much—not all of it good, of course, but by no means all of it bad—Murray's words have the

---

[5] D'Elia and Krason, *We Hold These Truths and More*, vii.

sound of an epitaph for the vision that had once led their author to argue for the existence of a deep compatibility between Catholicism and Americanism. Much now depends on how, and even whether, John Courtney Murray's vision can be retrieved and revived.

FLANNERY O'CONNOR
(1925–1964)

"I Cannot Afford to Be Less than an Artist"

As a richly gifted American fiction writer of the late twentieth century, Flannery O'Connor was not an evangelist
but an artist. Yet a profound Christian theological vision
informs her artistic vision, giving her stories a resonance that
sounds deep—and sometimes deeply disturbing—spiritual
chords. Which is exactly what their intensely Catholic
author meant these remarkable tales to do. "I am no disbe-
liever in spiritual purpose and no vague believer," O'Connor explained in a 1957 essay. "I see from the standpoint of
Christian orthodoxy. This means that for me the meaning
of life is centered in our Redemption by Christ and that
what I see in the world I see in its relation to that. I don't
think that this is a position that can be taken halfway."[1]

As for why she often wrote about grotesque characters in bizarre situations, O'Connor remarked that in this
present age of disbelief "you have to make your vision
apparent by shock—to the hard of hearing you shout, and
for the almost blind you draw large and startling figures."
Another time she said, "All my stories are about the action
of grace on a character who is not very willing to support
it." Then, with her characteristic mix of ruefulness and

[1] Unless otherwise noted, quotations are from Sally Fitzgerald, ed., *Flannery
O'Connor: Collected Works* (New York: Library of America, 1988).

realism, she added, "But most people think of these stories as hard, hopeless, brutal, etc."

Today, more than a half century after her death, that reaction to O'Connor's writing is more and more giving way to the realization that these are vividly imagined analogies of faith flung in the face of skeptical secularism by a master storyteller. Novelist and short story writer Joyce Carol Oates cites O'Connor's "unshakable absolutist faith" as the foundation of her creative work. Faith, said Oates, provided O'Connor with "a rationale with which to mock both her secular and bigoted Christian contemporaries in a succession of short stories that read like parables of human folly confronted by mortality".[2]

There was little in her family background and early life to suggest that here was a budding artist of note. The only child of a real-estate agent named Edward F. O'Connor and Regina Cline O' Connor, Mary Flannery O'Connor was born March 25, 1925, in Savannah, Georgia. Her great-grandparents were Irish immigrants, and the family had remained staunchly Catholic, members of a religious minority in the Protestant Bible Belt. As a child, Mary Flannery attended parochial schools until her father's failing health forced a move to the Cline family home in Milledgeville, Georgia. There she attended Peabody High School, drawing cartoons and writing for the school paper. In 1942, she entered Georgia State College for Women, an institution located near her home. It was then that she began to use the name Flannery O'Connor on school assignments. She graduated with a degree in social science.

In 1946, she was accepted by the prestigious Writers' Workshop at the University of Iowa and went there to

[2]Joyce Carol Oates, "The Parables of Flannery O'Connor", *The New York Review of Books*, April 9, 2009.

study journalism. While at Iowa she met important writers like Robert Penn Warren and John Crowe Ransom, began writing fiction, and started attending daily Mass. After Iowa, she spent time at the Yaddo Foundation artists' colony near Saratoga, New York, writing and socializing with writers who included the poet Robert Lowell, and attending Mass with the domestic staff.

Taken ill in 1950 while traveling home for Christmas, O'Connor was diagnosed with disseminated lupus erythematosus, the inflammatory connective tissue disease that had killed her father. She moved home for good and lived with her mother, settling into a routine of writing, tending her collection of peacocks and other exotic birds, exchanging letters with a growing number of correspondents, going to church with her mother, now and then lecturing on college campuses, and battling lupus.

She viewed her illness with cool courage, touched by humor. "I had a blood transfusion Tuesday," she wrote a friend not long before her death, "so I am feeling sommut better and for the last two days I have worked one hour each day and my my I do like to work. I et up that one hour like it was filet mignon."

Her first novel, *Wise Blood*, appeared in 1952 and received respectful but sometimes puzzled reviews. The story, she later told one of her correspondents, is about a "Protestant saint," Hazel Motes by name, "written from the point of view of a Catholic." Her second novel, *The Violent Bear It Away*, about a reluctant teenage prophet named Tarwater, came out in 1960. At the center of the tale is a struggle for the soul of a mentally handicapped boy pitting Tarwater against a nonbelieving secular intellectual. Between the novels, she produced a slow but steady stream of short fiction that appeared in places like *Kenyon Review, Sewanee Review, Harper's Bazaar*, and *Partisan Review*. The stories were collected in two volumes, *A Good Man Is Hard to Find* (1952) and the posthumously published *Everything That Rises Must Converge* (1965).

The unraveling of hypocrisy is a favorite theme with O'Connor, and a story called "Revelation" is a particularly striking example. Mrs. Turpin, a middle-aged farm woman possessed of sublime self-satisfaction and a keen eye for the faults of those she considers her inferiors, gets the shock of her life when a crazed girl in a doctor's office flings a book at her, tries to choke her, and tells her, "Go back to hell where you came from, you old wart hog."

It's the start of Mrs. Turpin's conversion. That evening, as she stands beside her hog pen, the conversion comes to completion in the vision of a "vast horde of souls" mounting to heaven. Leading the way are many of those she's been accustomed to look down on. Bringing up the rear are people like her. "They were marching behind the others with great dignity, accountable as they had always been for good order and common sense and respectable behavior.... Yet she could see by their shocked and altered faces that even their virtues were being burned away."

Mrs. Turpin walks slowly back to the house. The crickets are singing loudly in the woods, "but what she heard were the voices of the souls climbing upward into the starry field and shouting hallelujah."

Beyond routine hypocrisy, O'Connor sometimes confronts monstrous evil that might reasonably be described as demonic. In "A Good Man Is Hard to Find", an escaped killer called the Misfit slaughters a family whose grandmother confronts him at the end.

"No pleasure but meanness," he snarls at her.

She saw the man's face twisted close to her own as if he were going to cry and she murmured, "Why you're one of

my babies. You're one of my own children." She reached
out and touched him on the shoulder. The Misfit sprang
back as if a snake had bitten him and shot her three times
through the chest.

"She would have been a good woman," [he tells his
companions,] "if it had been somebody there to shoot her
every minute of her life."

O'Connor rejected the stereotyped explanation that she
wrote as she did because this was how writers of the so-
called Southern Gothic school wrote. Instead:

> My own feeling is that writers who see by the light of their
> Christian faith will have, in these times, the sharpest eyes
> for the grotesque, for the perverse, and for the unaccept-
> able.... The novelist with Christian concerns will find in
> modern life distortions which are repugnant to him, and
> his problem will be to make these appear as distortions to
> an audience which is used to seeing them as natural; and
> he may well be forced to take ever more violent means
> to get this vision across to this hostile audience.

In 1960, the Dominican Servants of Relief for Incurable
Cancer, a religious order of women founded by Nathan-
iel Hawthorne's daughter Rose, who operated a cancer
home in Atlanta, approached her with the request that she
write a book about a girl with a disfiguring facial tumor
whom the sisters had sheltered until her death at the age
of twelve. The sisters were deeply impressed by the girl's
courage and good spirits and wanted the world to know
about her. O'Connor told them they should write the
book themselves, but she negotiated its publication and
wrote the introduction. The volume appeared in 1961
as *A Memoir of Mary Anne*. Reflecting its author's own
bitter experience, her introduction is an extraordinary tes-
timony of faith.

"One of the tendencies of our age is to use the suffering of children to discredit the goodness of God," she wrote, "and once you have discredited His goodness, you are done with Him." In earlier times, people viewed unmerited suffering with "the blind, prophetical, unsentimental eye of acceptance, which is to say, of faith". But now "we govern by tenderness"—tenderness divorced from its source in Christ—which "ends in forced labor camps and in the fumes of the gas chamber". Today, perhaps, she would add abortion clinics to that list.

Shortly before entering the hospital for the last time in late July 1964, she learned that "Revelation" had won first prize in that year's O. Henry Awards competition. She died shortly after midnight on August 3 at the age of thirty-nine. The cause of death was kidney failure brought on by lupus. Her posthumous *Complete Stories* received the National Book Award for Fiction in 1972. Today her reputation continues to grow.

As a Catholic, a Southerner, and a chronic sufferer from a serious disease that eventually killed her, Flannery O'Connor had direct, personal experience of several kinds of distancing, not to say alienation, from the world of secular America at midcentury. She was therefore more than a little provoked by a *Life* magazine editorial complaining that current American fiction writers, the producers of a "hot-house literature", failed to mirror the prosperity and social progress of their country and indeed "the joy of life itself". O'Connor responded with the essay "The Fiction Writer and His Country", published in 1957, that offers a powerful insight into the springs of her own work.

As for Southern writers, she remarked, "We are all known to be anguished." But this, she quickly added, was not as a consequence of alienation from the rest of the country but arose from the fact that the South was "not alienated enough". The problem, in other words, was that "every day we are getting more like the rest of the country ... being forced out, not only of our many sins but of our few virtues."

Turning to the alienation imposed by faith, she suggested that the writer who is a religious believer "may at least be permitted to ask if these screams for joy would be quite so piercing if joy were really more abundant in our prosperous society". Not only that: the writer who nonetheless tries to oblige those who demand the writing of joyful fiction is likely to end up producing "a soggy, formless, and sentimental literature, one that will provide a sense of spiritual purpose for those who connect the spirit with romanticism and a sense of joy for those who confuse that virtue with satisfaction".

O'Connor continued to pursue this argument and brought it to a rousing conclusion in a second essay of 1957, "The Church and the Fiction Writer". Here she makes what is the definitive argument against the kind of assimilation that would require Catholic writers (or Catholic filmmakers or broadcasters or journalists or mail carriers or politicians or college professors or entrepreneurs or lawyers or scientists or physicians or accountants or business executives or anything else) to shed the fundamental elements of Catholic identity for the sake of acceptance by the secular culture on its spiritually impoverished terms rather than the terms of faith. She writes:

> The Catholic writer, in so far as he has the mind of the Church, will feel life from the standpoint of the central Christian mystery: that it has, for all its horror, been found by God to be worth dying for. But this should enlarge not narrow his field of vision.... The Catholic who does not write for a limited circle of fellow Catholics will in all probability consider that, since this is his vision, he

is writing for a hostile audience, and he will be more than ever concerned to have his work stand on its own feet and be complete and self-sufficient and impregnable in its own right. When people have told me that because I am a Catholic, I cannot be an artist, I have had to reply, ruefully, that because I am a Catholic I cannot afford to be less than an artist.

And she was not.

A half century ago Flannery O'Connor already knew from experience what it meant to be a faithful Catholic writer in secular America ("he is writing for a hostile audience") and adopted a strategy for dealing with it: to be the best artist she could. Few of the rest of us have either her vision or her artistry. That being the case, we can only pray: God grant us O'Connor's faith and the wit to find strategies of our own.

AFTERWORD

A Faithful Remnant?

Readers may wonder why this book ends where it does instead of going on to consider more recent figures in the American Catholic story. Don't people like Thomas Merton, Joseph Cardinal Bernardin, and Father Theodore Hesburgh, C.S.C., also qualify as influential American Catholics?

Certainly they do. But it's too soon for making the judgments required to fit them into the conceptual framework of this book. When, some time in the future, someone else writes another book about significant American Catholics, Merton, Bernardin, Hesburgh, and others will be parts of it.

For by no means has the story told here reached its end. Make no mistake, though: its recent chapters—ever more assimilation of Catholics into an ever more hostile American culture, ever more institutional and religious decline by the Church—have become steadily more ominous. We are nearing the point at which the American culture of which Catholics for so long have wanted so badly to be part replicates the culture described in a vivid passage of Saint Paul's letter to the Ephesians. In the pungent Knox translation: "Their minds are clouded with darkness; the hardness of their hearts breeds in them an ignorance, which estranges them from the divine life; and so, in despair, they

have given themselves up to incontinence, to selfish habits of impurity" (Eph 4:18–20).

I was speaking of these matters a while back to a Jewish journalist who replied that American Judaism has similar assimilation-related problems. Orthodox Jews, she said, are the only group in American Judaism now holding their own. On the Catholic side, one recalls a well-publicized remark by the late Francis Cardinal George, O.M.I., whom I quoted in the introduction to this book concerning the growing secularist onslaught against traditional Catholicism. Shortly before his retirement in 2014, the archbishop of Chicago said he expected to die in his bed, his successor as archbishop of Chicago to die in jail, and the successor's successor to be martyred in public. Later the cardinal explained that he was exaggerating to make a point. Plainly he succeeded in making it.

Walker Percy, another great Catholic who deserves a place in a future book like this one, put the matter about as hopefully as now reasonably can be done; he wrote that the time might be coming "when the Catholic Church and the Catholic people, both priest and laymen, will have become a remnant, a saving remnant, and that will be both bad news and good news".

The bad news is that the familiar comfort of the parish in which the Church was taken to be more or less co-extensive with the society ... is probably going or gone. The good news is that in becoming a minority in all countries, a remnant, the Church also becomes a world church in the true sense, bound to no culture, not even to the West of the old Christendom, by no means triumphant but rather a pilgrim church witnessing to a world in travail and yet a world to which it will appear ever stranger and more outlandish. It, the Church, will be

seen increasingly as what it was in the beginning, a saving remnant, a sign of contradiction, a transcultural phenomenon, a pilgrim church.[1]

If it comes to that—and it seems entirely possible it will—the situation of American Catholicism will certainly be bad, yet it also will hold a certain amount of tenuous promise. At least the remnant will be faithful, and something good might come of that. In God's mysterious, benevolent providence, it could be the starting point for a fresh beginning in the old story of American Catholics, their Church, and their nation.

[1] Walker Percy, "A 'Cranky Novelist' Reflects on the Church", in *Signposts in a Strange Land*, ed. Patrick H. Samway, S.J. (New York: Farrar, Straus and Giroux, 1991), 319–20.